THEATRE AS
SIGN-SYSTEM

THEATRE AS SIGN-SYSTEM

A semiotics of text and performance

Elaine Aston
and
George Savona

London and New York

First published 1991
by Routledge
11 New Fetter Lane, London EC4P 4EE

Simultaneously published in the USA and Canada
by Routledge
a division of Routledge, Chapman and Hall, Inc.
29 West 35th Street, New York, NY 10001

Typeset in 10/12 Palatino by
Falcon Typographic Art Ltd., Edinburgh & London
Printed in Great Britain by
Clays Ltd., St Ives plc

British Library Cataloguing-in-Publication Data
Aston, Elaine
Theatre as sign-system: a semiotics of text and performance.
1. Drama. Semiotics
I. Title   II. Savona, George
808.2

Library of Congress Cataloging-in-Publication Data
Aston, Elaine.
Theatre as sign-system: a semiotics of text and performance/
Elaine Aston, George Savona.
p. cm.
Includes bibliographical references.
1. Theater – Semiotics.   2. Drama – History and criticism.
I. Savona, George.   II. Title.
PN2041.S45A85   1991
792'.014 – dc20   91–9518

ISBN 0–415–04931–8
ISBN 0–415–04932–6 (paper)

For
June and Peter Aston
Alice and Jake Savona

CONTENTS

LIST OF FIGURES
AND TABLES

FIGURES

TABLES

ACKNOWLEDGEMENTS

For permission to quote from copyright material the authors would like to thank the following: Faber & Faber Ltd for the extracts from *Krapp's Last Tape* by Samuel Beckett, in *Krapp's Last Tape and Embers* (1965 edition); Penguin Books for the quotations from *The Cherry Orchard*, in *Plays: Chekhov* (translated by Elisaveta Fen, Penguin Classics, 1959, translation copyright Elisaveta Fen, 1951), *Hedda Gabler* in *Hedda Gabler and Other Plays*, by Henrik Ibsen (translated by Una Ellis-Fermor, Penguin Classics, 1950, translation copyright Estate of Una Ellis-Fermor, 1950), and *Oedipus the King*, in *The Three Theban Plays* by Sophocles (translated by Robert Fagles, Penguin Classics, 1984, translation copyright Robert Fagles, 1982, 1984).

The authors would also like to thank Tadeusz Kowzan for his kind permission to reproduce his revised classification of sign-systems (originally published in 1968, revised 1975) and *New Theatre Quarterly* for permission to reprint the questionnaire in 'Theatre Analysis: Some Questions and a Questionnaire', by Patrice Pavis, translated by Susan Bassnett (*NTQ*, 1, (2), May 1985: 205–8). A further note of thanks goes to Oliver Taplin whose *Greek Tragedy in Action* (Methuen, London, 1978, revised 1985) suggested the table in Chapter 2 (Table 2.1: Entrances and exits: *Oedipus the King*).

Finally, the authors would like to extend their thanks to the research committee of Nene College, Northampton, for supporting the project during the 1989–90 academic year; to Ed and Peter Green who helped to create the time and space for this book to be written; and to Gabriele Griffin, for her friendship.

Elaine Aston
George Savona

1

INTRODUCTION

WHY THEATRE SEMIOTICS?

Before mapping out the ground we propose to cover in this study, we need at the outset to clarify our own position in relation to theatre semiotics. Fundamentally, we view theatre semiotics not as a theoretical position, but as a *methodology*: as a way of working, of approaching theatre in order to open up new practices and possibilities of 'seeing'.

This is not, however, a view which has been widely held either by theatre departments in higher education or by the theatrical profession at large. 'Theatre Semiotics: An "Academic Job Creation Scheme?"', for example, was the provocative title of Brean Hammond's retrospective reflection upon the theatre conference held at Crewe and Alsager College in 1983 (1984). This title hints at the palpable hostility towards semiotics expressed both by a number of the conference panellists, who came from the academic world and the theatrical profession, and by participants speaking from the floor. Given this persistent and broad-based attack, one is tempted to ask, Why a book on theatre semiotics?

At one level, some of the criticism which theatre semiotics attracts is, in our view justified. The dangers of establishing a jargon-laden language accessible only to academics, of a dialogue between theoreticians and theoreticians, have not always been heeded. Martin Esslin (post-Alsager, a born-again semiotician) laments as follows in his preface to *The Field of Drama*: 'What struck me as unfortunate, however, from the outset, was the obscure language and excessively abstract way in which the, in many cases, outstandingly brilliant exponents of semiotics presented their findings' (1987: 11). The degree of

1

obfuscation has been such that the benefits of the 'findings', of understanding theatre as a sign-system, have tended to be eclipsed and the considerable advantages of studying theatre through a semiotic approach overlooked. It is our intention, therefore, to provide in this volume an introduction or guide to some of the most useful 'findings' theatre semiotics has to offer, and to do so in relatively straightforward terms. Furthermore, it is important at the outset both to identify what it is that theatre semiotics is reacting against and to indicate what its uses are.

In most academic institutions drama has, until relatively recently, been taught as a branch of literary studies, as dramatic literature and hence as divorced from the theatrical process. Such approaches to reading a play as were generally on offer did not significantly differ from the ways in which students were called upon to read a poem or a work of prose fiction, i.e. as literary objects. At best, a student might be invited to become an armchair critic or to imagine a theatrical space in her or his 'mind's eye'. Rarely, however, did drama leave the written page. Neither did discussion move beyond the boundaries of the text, in which characters were 'read' as 'real' people (and by implication could be psychoanalysed as such), and in which the key objective became the identification and analysis of a play's literary qualities, in order to establish what a play 'meant' via the reflexive application of the intentional fallacy. Theatrical consideration did not enter the frame of theoretical or critical practice.

The imposition of such approaches has proved singularly negative for the advancement of theatre studies, inasmuch as they fail to consider drama in its theatrical context: as a work which exists not only to be read but also to be *seen*. To examine a play for its literary qualities alone ignores its fundamental function as blueprint for production, a theatrical event which is to be realised in two planes (time and space), not one. Once the 'doing' of theatre is reinstated, then the notion of individual authorship is also challenged, given that the 'doing' also requires the collaboration of the performers, director(s), technical staff, and so on, all of whom contribute to the making of the theatrical event. At this point, one begins to grasp the plurality and complexity of the theatrical process, and to understand why it has been easier to abandon or relegate theatre to the province of dramatic literature for so long.

It was only when twentieth-century thought and approaches to literature and language radically shifted from the traditions of the nineteenth – the shift crudely recognised as the move from the 'what' to the 'how' – and attempted to understand the structures of 'artistic' language, that the primacy of the focus on the aesthetics and thematics of the text was displaced. This shift was achieved through the advent and development of what are now recognised as structural and semiotic approaches to literature (a brief history of which is offered below). The structuralist focus on the 'parts' of a work that make up a 'whole', and the semiotic enquiry into how meaning is created and communicated through systems of encodable and decodable signs, have changed the nature and function of literary criticism, in theory and in practice, and have had wide-ranging implications for all three literary genres: for poetry and prose, as well as drama. In the case of drama, this has involved both the development of new ways of interrogating the text and the generation of a methodology or 'language' with which to tackle the complexity of the theatrical sign-system. In this study we propose to document both of these areas, to see *how* meaning is generated through the elements involved in the scripting of drama, and *how* meaning is created within a performance context.

Linking the semiotic approaches under examination to specific dramatic texts and performances is, in our view, a vital way of avoiding the problems of obfuscation which were cited in the opening paragraphs of this introduction. Where the analysis of theatre as a sign-system has become divorced from the object of its enquiry, i.e. theatre, the sense of difficulty and frustration is intensified, and rejection of the semiotic approach is likely to follow. Two earlier studies which propose dramatic and theatrical analysis, J.L. Styan's *The Dramatic Experience* (1971 [1965]) and Ronald Hayman's *How to Read a Play* (1977), texts which still have currency as introductions to theatre, are written in seeming ignorance of the relevance of semiotics to theatre studies, despite the development of this approach since the turn of the century. This rejection is further reflected in the cross-section of recently published works which come under the umbrella of how-to-study-theatre

3

guides, and which equate accessibility with a rejection of the semiotic 'how' and demonstrate an empiricist return to the seemingly unproblematic 'what' (see Griffiths 1982, Kelsall 1985, Reynolds 1986).

As the impetus for a semiotic enquiry into theatre has derived primarily from continental Europe, the difficulty of establishing and developing theatre semiotics in English-speaking countries has been exacerbated by the problems of translation. Difficult terminology is compounded by the need to find equivalents in translation, thereby unhelpfully increasing the number of new terms brought into the semiotic vocabulary. Aside from reception difficulties, certain key texts have remained untranslated, thereby hindering the advancement of the field (see Bassnett 1984: 38–9). Or, when these are finally translated, the field may have moved on, and what may appear to some as a startling revelation is already viewed by others as *passé*. The one, seminal, study which has attempted to outline both the history of theatre semiotics and current areas of theory and practice for an English readership is Keir Elam's *The Semiotics of Theatre and Drama*, published in 1980. While this has filled a need for published documentation of theatre semiotics, it has nevertheless been greeted by students of theatre at first-degree level or below, as complex, difficult, and obscure to the point of inaccessibility. In the wake of Elam's publication, attempts to match accessibility with a mapping out of the semiotic field, such as Esslin's *The Field of Drama*, have unfortunately proved simplistic, reductive, and ultimately misleading. It is with these reservations in mind that we have set ourselves the task of achieving a more productive balance: to be both readable and informative.

The reply to 'Why theatre semiotics?' perhaps needs one final word of defence. Practitioners have constantly queried the need for a semiotic methodology of theatre, since this is viewed by them as a wholly academic enterprise. Hammond's post-seminar article summarised the view of the practitioners John Caird (director) and Peter Flannery (dramatist) who claimed 'that they had never heard of theatre semiotics before the Seminar and that they were none the wiser now that they had – they could do their jobs quite nicely without it, thank you' (Hammond 1984: 78). Of course, there would be no attempt on our part to argue that a grasp of semiotic theory is essential to

4

the making of effective pieces of theatre. However, whether we are involved in the making of theatre or whether we go to the theatre as spectators, the usefulness of the approach lies in its potential to make us more aware of *how* drama and theatre *are made*. As so much of British theatre operates as a commercial enterprise, the rationale for putting on plays is often reduced wholly to financial considerations, with an inevitable emphasis on product rather than process. The aim is to be successful (in commercial terms), not meaningful (in artistic/creative terms). Rehearsal techniques rooted in the blocking of moves and the learning of lines and little else are responsible for so much of what Peter Brook has identified as the all too prevalent mode of 'deadly theatre' (1968). Moreover, if we are in the business of 'seeing' theatre, whether for academic or professional or recreational purposes, surely we need a base from which to assess what we have seen? How often, when leaving a theatre, do we hear an uncertain voice saying, 'Well, I liked the scenery', or 'The costumes were nice'? Adopting an approach which invites us to look at the *how* can only serve to make us more aware of the potential of drama and theatre, whatever our interest, and more critical of how that potential is being ignored or abused.

STRUCTURALISM AND SEMIOTICS: A BRIEF HISTORY

At the turn of this century a new approach to the study of language was pioneered by the Swiss linguist, Ferdinand de Saussure. His *Course in General Linguistics*, published posthumously in 1915, advocated a structural study involving both the *diachronic* (historical) and *synchronic* (current) dimensions of language. Saussure's binary approach to the structural properties of language further posited the distinction between *langue* and *parole*, a duality which has remained central to structuralist approaches and has been simplified to an understanding of language (in the abstract, i.e. as system) and speech (as concrete utterance). What emerged from Saussure's work was an understanding of language as a sign-system, in which the linguistic sign was further presented in binary terms as *signifier*

5

and *signified* or 'sound-image' and 'concept'. The two sides of the linguistic sign are arbitrary, which enables language to be a self-regulating, abstract system, capable of transformation. It is through the interplay of similarities and differences between signifiers that meaning is created, and, in order to understand this, a structuralist approach is required in which the 'parts' of language are considered in relation to the 'whole'. In the light of this, it may be understood that language is the sign-system by which people mediate and organise the world.

A second turn-of-the-century pioneer in the field of sign-systems was the American philosopher, Charles S. Peirce. From Peirce's work on the complex way in which we perceive, and communicate in, the world by sign-systems, his classification of sign-functions has proved the most important and widely cited legacy in the field of theatre semiotics. His second 'trichotomy' of signs consists of: (i) *icon*: a sign linked by similarity to its object, e.g. a photograph; (ii) *index*: a sign which points to or is connected to its object, e.g. smoke as an index of fire; (iii) *symbol*: a sign where the connection between sign and object is agreed by convention and there is no similarity between object and sign, e.g. the dove as a symbol of peace. Some of the earlier semiotic studies of theatre posited theatre as an iconic activity, or the actor as icon. However, subsequent analysis has pointed towards the difficulties of attempting to adhere rigidly to these categories when it is clear that theatrical signs are characterised by overlap and complexity (see Elam 1980: 22–7).

Structuralist thinking was further advanced in the early twentieth century by the school of literary criticism identified as Russian Formalism. It was suppressed in the 1930s, given the growth of Marxist criticism and its emphasis on the sociological, but not before its two centres, the Moscow Linguistic Circle and the Petrograd Society for the Study of Poetic Language (OPOYAZ), had established a significant legacy for linguistic and literary studies. The Formalists – who included Boris Eichenbaum, Roman Jakobson, Victor Shklovsky and Boris Tomasjevsky – were primarily concerned with literary structures, and distinguished between 'poetic' or 'artistic' language and 'ordinary' language in an attempt to show the construction of 'literariness' (*literaturnost*). Central to this was the notion that art exists to reawaken our perception of life, the means to achieving this posited as the process of defamiliarisation: 'Art exists that one may recover the sensation of life; it exists to make one feel things, to make the stone *stony*' (Shklovsky 1965a: 12). This theoretical proposition was complemented by practical application, as demonstrated, for example, in Shklovsky's analysis of Sterne's *Tristram Shandy* (1921), which set out to expose the processes of defamiliarisation via an examination of Sterne's treatment of the erotic and of his use of time shifts.

In terms of theatre practitioners, the theory and practice of Bertolt Brecht has most clearly illustrated the formalist notion of 'making strange'. Brecht's notion of the *Verfremdungseffekt* (strategies for creating an effect of alienation in the actor and spectator) is directly derived from formalist notions of foregrounding or 'making strange': 'A representation that alienates is one which allows us to recognize its subject, but at the same time makes it seem unfamiliar' (Brecht 1964: 192). Brecht's techniques of defamiliarisation were ways of making strange the sign-systems of theatre. The actor who changes costumes on stage, performs with the house lights up or steps outside of her/his role to comment on it, defamiliarises our habits of theatrical 'seeing'.

One of the most important legacies of the formalist movement was Vladimir Propp's *Morphology of the Folktale*, which came out in Russia in 1928. Propp applied formalist methodology to a selection of fairy tales with the aim of establishing a taxonomy or 'grammar' for the fairy tale structure based on character *function*. The notion of being able to identify an underlying 'grammar' for the fairy tale was also to have structural implications for narrative in general (see Hawkes 1977: 67–9). In terms of theatre, the later work by the structuralist A.J. Greimas, whose notion of *actants* clearly derives from Propp, has had a more direct influence on the ways in which we read/see character since it has been widely applied in semiotic studies of dramatic texts (in particular, see Ubersfeld 1978).

It is against this early twentieth-century backdrop of formalist thinking that the notion of theatre as sign-system begins to emerge: most significantly, in the first instance, in the pioneering work of the Prague School in the 1930s and 1940s (see Chapter 6). The practitioners of the Prague School applied a semiotic methodology to artistic activity of all kinds. Attention was given to several forms of theatre (e.g. folk theatre, Chinese theatre) in an attempt to map out questions and areas of enquiry fundamental to this new way of seeing. Practitioners of the Prague School were concerned with a semiotics of both text and performance, and relations between the two. Jiři Veltruský's pioneering 'Dramatic Text as Component of Theater' (1976 [1941]), for example, sought to map out the relations and tensions between the linguistic sign-system of the dramatic text and the sign-system of the performance context.

What encouraged the advancement of the early structuralist and semiotic approaches to theatre in this period, was, as František Deák's retrospective article recounts (1976), the existence of an extensive corpus of theatrical material for the theoreticians to work on, in conjunction with the recognition and setting up of theatre as a theoretical and aesthetic object of study. In respect of the latter, Otakar Zich's *The Esthetics of Dramatic Art* (1931) is quoted (both historically and currently) as a seminal influence (see Deák 1976: 84). In seeking to understand the components of theatre and the relations between them, the Czech theoreticians established the premise that everything in the theatrical frame is a sign, that 'dramatic performance is a set of signs' (Honzl 1976: 74). It was recognised that objects placed on stage acquire greater significance than in the everyday world, that 'on the stage things that play the part of theatrical signs can in the course of the play acquire special features, qualities, and attributes that they do not have in real life' (Bogatyrev 1976: 35–6). The complexity of the theatrical sign-system and its capacity for change was located both as the enriching quality of theatre, but also the characteristic which made it so hard to define: 'I [Honzl] wanted to demonstrate the changeability that makes stage art so varied and all-attractive but at the same time so elusive of definition' (Honzl 1976: 93).

The importance of this structuralist and semiotic *modus operandi*, in changing twentieth-century ways of artistic thinking, cannot be overestimated. The extent of its influence may be seen by the way in which it has informed other disciplines or areas of study, such as the later work of the structuralist anthropologist, Claude Lévi-Strauss, on kinship relations and myth in primitive societies. By the 1960s a wide range of cultural, anthropological and literary activities had come under structuralist scrutiny and had consolidated the pioneering work of the first half of the twentieth century.

In respect of theatre, where the early semiotic work by the Prague School had concentrated on identifying rather than attempting to classify signs in the performance framework, semiotic approaches to theatre in the second part of this century have concentrated on schematising the early findings. Roland Barthes' comments on theatre in 'Literature and Signification' (1972 [1963]), opened with a description of theatre as 'a kind of cybernetic machine' and theatricality as *a density of signs*. He went on to propose a series of questions: How may we analyse this 'privileged semiological object'? What are the relations between the signs? How is meaning created in a theatrical production? 'How', he asked, 'is the theatrical signifier formed?' and, 'What are its models?' (261–2). These were questions to which other theatre semioticians sought answers. Attempts at classifying theatrical sign-systems were to follow: notably the taxonomy of the Polish semiotician, Tadeusz Kowzan in 'The Sign in the Theater' (1968) and, more recently, the classification devised for students by the French theatre semiotician, Patrice Pavis, in the form of a questionnaire (1985a). (Both these classifications will be examined in detail in Chapter 6.)

Semiotic work in the field of theatre has continued to advance. Elam's extensive bibliography of further reading suggestions in his 1980 volume points towards the number of semiotic studies published in relation to drama and the dramatic text, whilst highlighting the need for more work on the performance text/context. Currently, theatre departments in further and higher education are experiencing a practical need for students of theatre to become more proficient in the making (encoding) and reading (decoding) of performance text and contexts. We would argue, as the Prague theoreticians did, that both 'texts' should come under semiotic scrutiny. We propose the advancement and synthesis of the structuralist/semiotic legacy in order to approach theatre in a way which might be read as objective or 'scientific' (though certainly not reductive): to deconstruct the theatrical/dramatic processes in order to reawaken our perceptions of how theatre is made and read as a sign-system.

THE PROJECT

The form of the present book therefore reflects the two main fields of study: text and performance. We have proceeded from the view that semiotics has clear implications for the study of both dramatic and theatrical discourses. In the case of the former, it permits structural investigations of the dramatic text. With regard to the latter, it furnishes a metalanguage with which to analyse the pictorial, physical and aural 'languages' of theatre.

The first chapters (2–5) identify the underlying *how* of the dramatic text. We are concerned here with its principal elements and defining characteristics: form, character, dialogue modes and stage directions. Chapter 2 surveys approaches to the analysis of dramatic structure, examining the dramatic genres in terms of the formalist perception of the transformation of 'story' into 'plot'. This entails consideration of how drama is 'made', an exploration of the conditions of meaning-production which obtain for the dramatic text. We shall examine, for example, how plot is organised by means of act and scene divisions, and the conventions of 'openings' and 'closures', in order to demonstrate how drama arrives at recognisable generic and stylistic structures. Chapter 3 introduces the concept of character as *functional* in terms of plot, thus building on the work of the preceding chapter. The functional and actantial models of Propp and Greimas are used as the basis for our methodology here. While we are not concerned (other than for purposes of deconstruction) with traditional psychologising modes of enquiry, we shall review current applications of psychoanalytic theory to the study of character. Chapter 4 considers the range of dialogue modes operative within the dramatic text. Given that different genres and styles tend to draw on different modes and registers of dramatic dialogue, it is our intention to provide a systematic demonstration of the differential frequenting of the former by the latter. We wish to demonstrate, also, that in dramatic discourse characters are constructed wholly within and by means of language. Chapter 5 addresses stage directions. This is a particularly underdeveloped topic, and will be pursued further in Chapter 7. We begin with an overview of intra- and extra-dialogic directions, and then classify and examine the functions of the various types of direction. Of particular interest here are directions relating to the physical and vocal definition of character, and to design and technical elements. As in the previous chapter, with regard to dialogue we are concerned to demonstrate how specific types of direction are associated with specific dramatic and theatrical forms.

Chapters 6–9 chart the elements of performance. Chapter 6 lays the groundwork for the establishment of a 'language' with which to discuss the text in performance and examines attempts to classify theatre as a sign-system, the codification of the sign-system and the decodifying activity of the spectator. Chapter 7 returns to the subject of stage directions, in order to assess their implications for stage practice. Chapter 8 is concerned with the reading of images, considering how systems of staging (e.g., lighting, setting, conventions of acting) are deployed to construct stage pictures. We shall examine the levels of operation of stage pictures and indicate strategies whereby the pictures may be decoded. We shall look also at the serial development of stage picture into visual metaphor, as a device wherewith to counterpoint narrative line and/or to foreground ideological content, and at the implications of the written text for performance style. Chapter 9 offers a synthesis of the approaches to text and performance investigated in the previous chapters, combining methodology and practice in comparative readings of two filmed performances of Samuel Beckett's *Krapp's Last Tape* (1965).

As a methodology, theatre semiotics in its present state of development reveals certain shortcomings, and has yet to be applied systematically to a number of topics of interest to the present project, particularly in the area of performance. We shall seek to highlight both problems and undeveloped areas, and in the concluding chapter we signpost developments arising out of the semiotic approach. Finally, we offer an accompanying list of suggestions for further reading, annotated to enable the individual reader to follow up a particular aspect of theatre semiotics. For purposes of illustration, we shall draw upon a body of ten texts selected to cover a historic and generic spectrum appropriate to our project. These are as follows:

Sophocles	*Oedipus the King*	(trans. Fagles)	Penguin
Anon	*Everyman*		Everyman
Shakespeare	*As You Like It*		Methuen
Racine	*Phaedra*	(trans. Cairncross)	Penguin
Hazlewood	*Lady Audley's Secret*		OUP
Chekhov	*The Cherry Orchard*	(trans. Fen)	Penguin
Ibsen	*Hedda Gabler*	(trans. Ellis-Fermor)	Penguin
Brecht	*The Mother*	(trans. Gooch)	Methuen
Beckett	*Endgame*		Faber
Churchill	*Top Girls*		Methuen

(Unless otherwise indicated, passages quoted are referenced by page number and full details of editions used are cited in the bibliography.)

The texts are representative of the three historical phases of drama which we have identified as follows: (1) 'classic' (*Oedipus the King, Everyman, As You Like It, Phaedra*); (2) 'bourgeois' (*Lady Audley's Secret, The Cherry Orchard, Hedda Gabler*); (3) 'radical' (*The Mother, Endgame, Top Girls*). This three-phase developmental model will be drawn on where appropriate and beneficial to theoretical or methodological explanations.

It is hoped that the key semiotic 'findings' offered in either section of the book will enable the reader both to focus on specific aspects of dramatic or theatrical analysis which are of immediate interest to her/him, and to develop a broad-based understanding of theatre as a sign-system.

Part I
TEXT

[Part]

TEXT

2

DRAMATIC SHAPE

The development of structuralist analysis and the establishment
of semiotics as a field of study, as outlined in the introduction,
resulted in making the construction of the text and the processes of its signification visible. Working from a linguistic
base, formalists and structuralists proceeded to examine the
structural elements of texts, their combinations, relations and
codifications, in order to see how meaning is created via the
underlying systems of rules and conventions. Much of this
early work was centred on the processes of textual encoding.
A principal consideration was narratology and the possibility
of establishing a universal model or theory of narrative, as foregrounded, for example, in Barthes' 1966 essay, 'Introduction to
the Structural Analysis of Narratives' (collected in Barthes 1977:
79–124). Although models for types of texts were developed
(see Propp 1968, Greimas 1983, 1970), the possibility of desig-
nating literature as a science, implicit in formalist/structuralist
thinking and procedures, was subsequently subjected to a
self-reflexive critique. In our so-called post-structuralist era,
the emphasis has switched from the process of encoding to
that of decoding: to examining the active engagement between
the structures of text and the decodifying activity of the reader
(see Barthes 1975, Eco 1979). What follows is an 'untying' of
the text (Young 1981), a move away from the notion of the
text as a closed system to consideration of its unfixing in the
plurality of signifying processes generated through the activity
of reading/spectating.

In this chapter, the first of four devoted to the semiotics of the
dramatic text, we propose to consider the shaping of the dramatic text in respect of both encoding and decoding activities.

An examination of the closed system of formal properties whose function it is to shape and underpin the drama is a first step towards understanding how the text is made. Were this to be our only consideration, as it was for the early structuralists, our enterprise would indeed be reductive. Instead, the analysis of encoding processes must be linked to the ways in which signs of shape or form are actively decoded by the reader/spectator.

SIGNS OF DIVISION

One fundamental formal characteristic of drama is the method by which the content is organised into blocks of text. Where a novel traditionally does this by means of chapter divisions, drama is divided up into acts and/or scenes which signal the beginning and end of a unit of action in relation to the whole. These are, as Veltruský argues, 'a matter of convention' (1977: 82). Moreover, the conventions are linked to the evolution of generic and stylistic forms within the dramatic canon and may carry different functions for the writer and for the reader of the text.

For the dramatist, whilst it may be true that an idea for a play is sensed in advance of its composition, how that idea is given a dramatic shape depends upon the type of theatre the writer has in view. Dramatists are themselves readers and spectators of plays, and their own cultural and theatrical conditioning will interact with the process of dramatic composition.

At certain points in the history of drama and theatre the conventions of division have received critical or theoretical attention with the consequence that a particular age or period of drama has established a notion of an 'ideal' form. That so much of the Renaissance drama is written in a five-act structure, for instance, is neither arbitrary nor coincidental, but reflects a revival of interest in Greek and Roman drama. Or, if you will, a rigorous implementation of Horace's advice to dramatists: 'If you want your play to be called for and given a second performance, it should not be either shorter or longer than five acts' (1965: 85). That these theoretical 'ideals' do not exist in practice has not detracted from their serious influence on the art of play construction. Aristotle's description of tragedy (itself predicated upon the idealisation of the work of Sophocles' middle period) has provided a set of rules and conventions, still traceable in the nineteenth-century 'classic realist' tragedies of Ibsen despite their inability to provide an adequate structural model for the drama they originally purported to describe. Indeed, notions of an 'ideal' form have been such that theoreticians have seen fit to reorganise imperfections: the non-segmented comic complications of Terentian comedies, subsequently organised into a five-act structure by the classical grammarian Donatus, being a case in point.

For the reader, the division of a play into acts and scenes affects the reading of a script. A block of text presented as an act is offered both as a self-contained unit and as a link in the structural chain. We read to the end of an act and simultaneously match this moment of 'closure' with a wider view of the dramatic frame. This reading experience may however be radically different when the written text is seen. Where 'breaks' are signified to the reader by means of acts and scenes, in performance such divisions may not be apparent. The spectator, now unaware of the units of text, instead experiences continuity. In French classical tragedy, for example, the reader of the dramatic text is aware of the five-act structure and the regular marking of a new scene each time a character makes an exit or entrance. These conventions of play construction are not experienced in performance, where the playing of the action is continuous. Alternatively, other elements of staging in theatre may be used to signify a moment of 'closure', e.g. a lighting cue or the convention of raising and lowering the curtain at the beginning and end of an act.

In all of these three processes – the writing, reading and spectating of drama – the structural divisions are conventions which are learnt. They are part of the highly complex, rule-based principles of the dramatic text, established through the generic and stylistic evolutions of theatre and performance conditions.

CONSTRUCTION OF PLOT

Whilst act and scene divisions are 'a matter of convention', the process may be further understood as linked to 'the characteristic features of the dramatic plot' (Veltruský 1977: 82). Veltruský argues for the dependence of act unity and segmentation on the 'dramatic conflict on which the plot relies' (82). He illustrates his point by citation of an exception. His reference to the drama of Maeterlinck offers an example of play construction which does not follow the traditional graphic pattern of the rise and fall towards an inevitable conclusion, as demonstrated in the classic five-act structure. Maeterlinck's rejection of traditional external conflicts of drama in favour of dramatising the 'Tragical in Daily Life' is demonstrated by his organisation of units of text into tableaux, i.e. not 'great adventures' in a swiftly moving sequence of peripatetic action, but a lyrical painting of the deeper tragic element underlying day-to-day existence (1899: 97). Using the convention of tableaux as a means of textual division, therefore, signals a subversion of dramatic form (and, by implication, of content) to the reader, who adjusts her/his expectations accordingly.

Veltruský and other pioneering semioticians and formalists had been quick to recognise that a text which subverts expectations may usefully serve to reawaken our perceptions of literary construction and the devices which underpin it (for example, see Shklovsky 1965b). To reinforce this point, and to consolidate Veltruský's example from Maeterlinck, we could usefully cite a further example of a 'deviant' text which, through its abuse of dramatic conventions, draws our attention to sign-systems of structure. Beckett's *Waiting for Godot* is written in two acts, and, structurally, one would expect to find a unit of preparation, conflict and crisis, to be resolved in the second and final act or unit. Instead, Beckett offers a cyclical mirroring, a structural parallelism which does not advance dramatic conflict and which works to undermine our expectations of dramatic form. The pattern of the 'old' is used and subverted to create the 'new'.

It may therefore be deduced that, traditionally, the conventions of act and scene division work in tandem with the construction of the dramatic plot. They contribute to the shaping and signposting of the unified beginning, middle and end of drama. Since Aristotle's commentary on the 'unity of plot' and the description of its parts in Greek tragedy, analysis of plot construction has remained a constant site of critical enquiry. Descriptions of the graphic, classic structure have generally posited a tripartite model. A.C. Bradley's comments on the design of Shakespearean tragedy offer a model based on exposition, conflict and catastrophe (1961: 30). This outmoded form of analysis, which centres on dramatic conflict and opposing forces, still continues to inhibit the teaching of Shakespeare at secondary level and to unhelpfully inform current approaches to the construction of dramatic texts (for example, see Griffiths 1982).

Investigations into structure, even in a non-structuralist sense, may be useful in so far as they contribute to our insights into dramatic form. In the field of Greek tragedy, for example, structural readings have been many and varied. The anthropologically informed Cambridge school of classicists (Cook, Cornford, Farnell, Harrison *et al.*) looked to ritual to further their understanding of the tragic form, seeing tragedy as possibly related to a six-stage conjectural reconstruction of Dionysiac ritual: (1) Agon or contest, (2) Pathos or disaster, (3) Messenger, (4) Lamentation and possible rejoicing, (5) Discovery or recognition, (6) Epiphany or resurrection (Murray 1965: 30). Francis Fergusson worked from this concept of ritual to identify a further shaping model based on the 'tragic rhythm of action', again presented in three parts: Purpose, Passion and Perception (1965: 18). This represented both the structure of individual episodes and the overarching dramatic framework. More recently, Oliver Taplin's study of Greek drama (1985), which takes as its starting point the structural dynamics of chorus and actor units, has perhaps taught us more about the performance conditions of Greek theatre than any other modern approach (see Table 2.1).

Certain types of theatre may also foreground plot construction in the hierarchy of the linguistic sign-system. This is particularly true of drama where the characters have designated roles to play in the plot (see Chapter 3), as in the genres of melodrama or farce. Eugène Scribe's prolific output of popular drama (from the early part of the nineteenth century) established a particular form recognised as the *well-made play*. These plays were extremely successful with the audiences of their time, but were critically derided. Modern scholarship has reappraised their value as a popular theatre form and demonstrated that they may teach us much about plot construction. Stephen Stanton's structural description of the *well-made play* identifies seven features: plot, pattern of action and suspense, ups and downs of the hero's fortunes, counterpunch of peripeteia and *scène à faire*, central misunderstanding known to the spectators but not to the characters, logical denouement, and overall pattern of action replicated in individual acts (1957: xii–xiii). Stanton makes the point that Scribe was not offering anything new in all of this, but was plundering the devices of the classical comedy tradition (from Plautus, Molière, Beaumarchais, *et al.*) to create a form which relied structurally on logic and inevitability. What Scribe had identified, therefore, were the underlying elements of a structural 'grammar', out of which he was able to produce a highly successful dramatic formula. Types of texts which demonstrate recurring patterns of structural elements, such as the 'well-made play' or its successor the thesis or problem play, have been the subject of formalist and structuralist enquiries into narratology (see Chapter 3 on Propp and Greimas).

Alternatively, types of theatre which operate in a self-referential mode may 'make strange' the mechanics of dramatic plot by foregrounding devices of structure as a dominant sign of metatheatricality. The reworking of the classics towards a modern end, which characterises early twentieth-century French drama, self-consciously dispenses entirely with the question 'What is to happen?', and invites the reader to engage in a decoding of 'how' it will happen. To take one example, the prologue to Anouilh's *Antigone* identifies all the characters and their destinies before the 'action' begins. The 'story' is told as part of the 'plot' mechanism.

STORY AND PLOT

It follows that issues of dramatic structure have, at various times, been of interest to different critical schools of thought. Structuralist thinking, rooted in early twentieth-century formalism and developed in the 1960s, did not consider form as one of a number of aspects of literary enquiry, but proposed an understanding of all literature based on the network of underlying structural relations governing textual production. The distinction, first identified by the Russian Formalists in relation to *fabula* (story) and *sjuzet* (plot), has remained central to structuralist methodology. While early investigations along these lines were applied to prose fiction, the distinction holds true for the dramatic text also.

Essentially, story is the basic narrative outline; plot, the means by which narrative events are structured, organised and presented. For example, the story of Oedipus as narrated by the Greek myth, consists of a chronological outlining of events which befall Oedipus. Opening with the oracle before his birth, in which it is revealed to Laius and Jocasta that their son will kill the father and marry the mother, the story then proceeds to document consequential events *in the order in which they happen*. This 'covers several generations' and 'has as much narrative material as *Gone with the Wind*' (Fergusson 1968: 15). Sophocles' tragedy dramatises the end of the myth, replacing the linearity of the story-line with a plot which organises the events of years into twenty-four hours, reordering the chronology of the Oedipus biography according to the exigencies of a dramatic form dictated by the clue-feeding, detective structure which shapes the plot of the tragedy. In this way, the story is retold and resequenced, the original story-line becoming a shaped process of narration, which in performance is shared between the actors and the chorus.

The compression and concentration of plot-sequencing arises because, as Veltruský explains, the construction of the dramatic plot is 'graded' (1977: 77–8). This is highlighted 'whenever a story borrowed from narrative is used in drama', as in the Oedipus example. Whilst narrative works may also move away from a linear mode, Veltruský argues that such gradation is 'more loosely' based 'than in drama', suggesting that this becomes apparent in the transformation of a novel into a play. To illustrate Veltruský's point, and to further our understanding of dramatic plot construction, we can examine the transformation of *Lady Audley's Secret* from a 400-page narrative into a two-act drama.

As a society melodrama, *Lady Audley's Secret* in play form is an example of a dramatic genre in which plot is prioritised over character. Psychological detail furnished in the source novel is absent from the play, where characters are reduced to stereotypes: villainess, gulled widower, crafty servant, etc. Characters in the play are important not in terms of who they are, but for what they do. It is through the concentrated form of their actions that narrative events are retold and shaped into

21

the swiftly moving, peripatetic pattern of dramatic plot (see also Chapter 3 on character functions).

While the scope and breadth of the narrative plot allow for a leisurely and detailed consideration of character, it too has its own 'graded' structure, arising from the 'cliff-hanger' technique of serial writing. This relies on reordering the events of the story-line to partially reveal or to withhold information, in order to maintain the reader's suspense and to provoke curiosity with regard to the discovery of Lady Audley's secret. Yet (and this is Veltruský's point) it also employs the linear order of the story, as the reader follows the search of the 'detective' (Robert Audley) for clues to the secret, according to the chronology in which they are sought and found. This contrasts with the dramatic plot, where the reader is placed in a more informed position than the characters, chiefly through the use of information-giving monologues and asides. The latter function as a means to signify the divorce between public mask and private face, and serve to accentuate the unease underlying surface benignity. In turn, this creates a transference of dramatic suspense from the past of the villainess (revealed to the reader before it is discovered through events by the characters) to the question of whether the other protagonists will realise her true nature in time to arrest her evil actions. This again reflects the shift from psychology to action.

These general points of contrast may be further illustrated by considering one specific incident as it is treated in both the novel and the play: the murder of George Talboys:

(1) So the grey old building had never worn a more peaceful aspect than on that bright afternoon on which George Talboys walked across the lawn to ring a sonorous peal at the sturdy, iron-bound, oak door.

The servant who answered his summons told him that Sir Michael was out, and that my lady was walking in the lime-tree avenue.

He looked a little disappointed at this intelligence, and muttering something about wishing to see my lady, or going to look for my lady (the servant did not clearly distinguish his words), walked away from the door without leaving either card or message for the family.

It was full an hour and a half after this when Lady Audley

returned to the house, not coming from the lime-walk, but from exactly the opposite direction, carrying her open book in her hand, and singing as she came. Alicia had just dismounted from her mare, and stood in the low-arched doorway, with her great Newfoundland dog by her side.

The dog, which had never liked my lady, showed his teeth with a suppressed growl.

(Braddon 1985: 67)

(2) LADY AUDLEY. One moment. I will accompany you if you will let me be a few seconds to myself, so that I may send a few lines in my tablets to Sir Michael, saying I shall never see him more.

GEORGE. Well, be quick then. (*Music, piano, to end of act.*)

LADY AUDLEY. I will. (GEORGE *goes up, and as his back is turned she goes to the well, takes off the iron handle, and conceals it in her right hand behind her – aside.*) It is mine! that is one point gained – now for the second. (*Aloud, pretending faintness.*) Water, water, for mercy's sake! (GEORGE *comes down.*) My head burns like fire!

GEORGE. This is some trick to escape me; but I will not leave you.

LADY AUDLEY. I do not wish you. Stoop down and dip this in the well, (*gives him her white handkerchief*) that I may bathe my throbbing temples. (GEORGE *takes handkerchief and goes to well.*) Quick, quick!

GEORGE (*stooping down to well*). It is the last service I shall render you.

(LADY AUDLEY *creeps up behind him unperceived.*)

LADY AUDLEY (*striking him with the iron handle*). It is indeed – die! (*Pushes him down the well, the ruined stones fall with him.*) He is gone – gone! and no one was a witness to the deed!

LUKE (*looking on*, R.U.E.). Except me! (*Aside.*)

LADY AUDLEY (*exulting*). Dead men tell no tales! I am free! I am free! I am free! I am free! – Ha, ha, ha!
(*Raises her arms in triumph, laughing exultingly –* LUKE *looks on, watching her as the drop falls.*)

(247–8)

In the melodrama, the 'murder' of George Talboys constitutes the climactic moment of closure at the end of the first act. The on-stage murder is the logical and inevitable consequence of the preceding, cumulative commentary on the evil ways of Lady Audley. Because it is shown, the reader/spectator is placed in the position of a key witness to the crime. The melodramatic form dictates the constant shifts between triumphs and disasters to maintain the momentum of the plot. Hence Lady Audley's exultation over the death of her first husband and the absence of witnesses is immediately and ironically negated by the unseen figure of Luke (whose presence is of course witnessed by the spectator).

In the narrative plot, it is impossible for the reader to tell what has happened. The mode is enigmatic. There is a gap of one and a half hours in the narration. What has taken place is not clear, though some sinister event is conventionally signalled by the growling dog. As the narrative uses a past tense to report on events, it places the reader in the position of a detective having to reconstruct a crime from the limited information available.

The contrasting documentation of this event highlights the difference between the narrative mode of the novel and the mimetic, 'doing' mode of the play. Significant actions in the novel – the 'murder', George's reaction to Lady Audley's portrait, or the death of Luke – are shrouded in mystery, though directly presented at the moment they occur (in dramatic plot time) in the melodrama. This might lead one to suppose that the mimetic mode of drama lends itself to a non-distinction between story and plot, i.e. that drama consists simply of an acting out of the story-line. Elam raises this point, but goes on to answer it by affirming that 'the *sjuzet/fabula* distinction holds good for the drama' given that the representation of the dramatic world is 'non-linear, heterogeneous, . . . discontinuous . . . and incomplete' (1980: 119). Elam expands this assertion by demonstrating (and this he illustrates with reference to *Macbeth*) how (a) in drama, the logical ordering of the story-line is realised through different modes of representation, e.g. a narrative unit may be directly shown as part of the 'actual' world or reported after the event, and how (b) drama presents/acts out as part of its 'actual' world elements of plot which would not be included in a story outline. *Lady Audley's Secret* offers several examples which illustrate Elam's point. The Morris-dancing scene of Act I is part of the 'actual' world, but would not figure in a story-line. We are not shown Robert's search for his friend, as we are in the novel; it is simply reported during the course of a dialogue between Alicia and her father, at the opening of Act II, as having already taken place. Here too, the reader/spectator experiences a gap, signifying the incompleteness of the 'actual' world; six months have passed between Acts I and II. This is accepted as a matter of convention.

CONVENTIONS OF DRAMATIC PLOT AND TIME

It is the selection and combination of such conventions which structures the received or invented story-line into a dramatic plot. We can become more aware of the operation of conventions by reverting to an Aristotelian tripartite model for drama and re-examining characteristic plot elements by looking at the dominant features of the openings, developments and closures of plays, and by examining these in relation to the story/plot distinction and to the dramatic conventions of time.

Opening a play is a highly structured process, notwithstanding that the reader/spectator is positioned to receive it as a 'natural' beginning. Traditionally, a first scene needs to supply us with story-line information: setting the scene, introducing characters and establishing the beginnings of an action. In terms of the 'story', the play does not necessarily start at the beginning. *Oedipus the King*, for example, we noted as opening just before the close of the mythic narrative. The events depicted in the dramatic plot may represent a moment of action which is the result of a chronology of events in the dramatic past; events which have taken place before the play begins and which are reported as part of the opening. An opening frequently combines reported past events with current events in the 'actual' dramatic world which we are shown. The exposition between Oedipus and the Priest dramatises the immediate problem of the plague with a report of the past deeds of Oedipus: his encounter with the Sphinx and in consequence his deliverance of the city of Thebes. The fictional layers of the past are interwoven with the concerns of the dramatic present.

Past reporting between characters is a convention common to the tragic genre, where dramatic plots are centred on a particular moment of anxiety, and where the past is an inevitable and inescapable force weighing heavily on the characters. The use of unnamed 'servant' characters, in whom we are interested not for themselves but for what they have to tell us, may be used as one means of storytelling (see Veltruský 1977: 51; see Chapter 3 for further details). *Phaedra* opens with a conversation between Hippolytus and his confidant, Theramenes, a conversation which has already begun before the play opens. The use of a confidant(e) provides a means for a major, named character to reveal concerns and issues central to the unfolding of the tragic conflict. Twenty lines into *Phaedra*, we know that Theseus, the King, has been missing for over half a year, that extensive searches to find him have proved fruitless, and that Hippolytus is about to depart on a further search. These are story-line details represented through a formal convention of dramatic plot.

The proportion of the story revealed in an opening is largely dependent upon generic and stylistic factors. In the case of *Oedipus the King* and *Phaedra* the dramas are both myth-based and the story-line is therefore closed or fixed, and known to the reader. (For more on the notion of closed texts see Eco's piece on 'The Myth of Superman' in Eco 1979: 107–24). Interest therefore switches from what is to happen (story) to how it is to happen (plot). The enigmatic mode, characteristic of dramatic openings, in both cases depends on the gradual and partial revelation of anxieties and problems, known in terms of the myth/story but reordered in terms of plot, etc. In *Phaedra*, the opening dialogue feeds us clues of anxiety deriving from the circumstances of the main characters of the tragedy:

The King – Theseus – lost.

The Queen – Phaedra – seeking to die.

The Princess – Aricia – object of Hippolytus' love.

The story of each is told, and links are gradually established in preparation for the dramatic conflict to come. The more a reader knows of a character's story, the greater the opportunity for irony. In *Oedipus the King*, it is the King who searches for clues, whilst the informed reader knows that the seeker and the sought-for are one and the same. How Oedipus will discover (plot) what the reader already knows (story) constitutes the centre of dramatic interest.

Because the unfolding and development of a plot is graded and non-linear, drama draws on its formal conventions or properties to generate tension, suspense or interest in the rise-and-fall momentum of the plot structure. The dramatic shape of Sophocles' tragedy takes its form from a series of duologues between Oedipus and another named character or messenger/servant figure, interspersed with verses from the chorus. Using Taplin's scheme of entrances and exits (see Table 2.1) we observe at a glance how and when narrative information leading to the solution of the fatal riddle is fed into the plot structure. The duologues are designed to reveal a further clue, pushing the action on to its inevitable conclusion.

For example, when Jocasta enters to respond to the argument between Creon and Oedipus, she has a more important function: to report the beginning of the Oedipus story, i.e. the narrative concerning Laius and the oracle. Past and present collide when the Messenger enters to relate the death of Polybus in the dramatic present, and to demystify further 'facts' about the birth of Oedipus. The sequences involving the Chorus do not reveal story-line information, but comment upon it, reinforcing the dominant concerns of the tragedy. Their delivery marks a shift from the rhetorical to the lyrical, the histrionic to the choreographic, the individual to the group, and so on, which acts as a contrasting element in the plotting of the tragic action.

This sense of action being pushed on towards a fatal outcome derives, as Veltruský describes it, from the 'momentum of the dramatic plot', which he further links to the concept of time:

> Its progression [i.e. the progression of the dramatic plot] is bound up with the flow of time: once dramatic plot is set in motion, the flow of time alone is enough to make the reader feel that it progresses uninterruptedly and irresistibly, even when the flow of language weakens or stops altogether so that the flow of time becomes the sole vehicle of the progression of the plot.
>
> (1977: 80)

Time is a crucial element in plot construction, and functions in the following key ways:

1. Time present: the location of the spectator in the 'here and now' of a fictional universe which unfolds in the playing out of the dramatic action. This is experienced by the spectator as a continuous temporal plane, and it is one which is

Table 2.1. Entrances and exits: *Oedipus the King*

Entrances & Exits	Enter Oedipus from central door – attended: tableau of supplication	→ Priest acts as spokesman for the group	→ Priest announces arrival of Creon
Function of entrances/ exits	*To ask meaning of supplication*	*To ask Oedipus to deliver Thebes*	*To relate news from Delphic oracle*
General exit Oedipus goes into palace	→ Enter Chorus of Theban Elders	→ Enter Oedipus from palace	→ Enter Teiresias led by attendant
To await gathering of citizens as commanded	*Question: Will the problem be solved?*	*Comes to offer help/Announces has already sent for Teiresias*	*To name Oedipus as the polluter of Thebes*
Exit Teiresias & Oedipus	→ Chorus	→ Enter Creon	→ Enter Oedipus
Teiresias is dismissed: Oedipus is left with riddle to solve	*To comment on Teiresias' revelation*	*In response to Oedipus' accusations*	*To argue with Creon*
Enter Jocasta	→ Exit Creon	→ Exit Jocasta & Oedipus	→ Chorus
To respond to the argument	*Dismissed by Oedipus/Jocasta to reveal history of oracle*	*To await shepherd as sent for*	*To comment on human pride & the role of the gods*
Enter Jocasta	→ Enter Messenger	→ Enter Oedipus	→ Exit Jocasta
To make offerings to gods	*To relate news of death of Polybus & to reveal Oedipus is not the son of Polybus*	*Fetched by attendant to hear this news*	*To take her own life*
Chorus	→ Enter Shepherd	→ Exit Shepherd & Messenger	→ Chorus
To comment on mystery of parentage of Oedipus	*As sent for/ Identifies Oedipus as son of Laius & Jocasta*	*Functions complete*	*To lament on unhappy fate of man*

Table 2.1 continued

Enter Attendant →	Enter Oedipus →	Enter Creon →	Enter Ismene & Antigone
To report Jocasta's death & self-blinding of Oedipus	*To lament with Chorus*	*To take up rule*	*As final request of Oedipus*
Exit Oedipus →	Chorus		
To await judgement of gods	*Final homily on unhappy condition of man*		

frequently 'pointed to', especially during opening sequences which serve to locate the spectator in the 'here and now' (e.g. temporal references to Irina's 'name-day' in the opening sequence to Chekhov's *Three Sisters*, or to establish the time of day in the first lines of *The Cherry Orchard*).

2. Chronological time: the linear time sequence of the story (*fabula*). This constitutes the chronological time-scale of events, i.e. events as they occur in the narrative order.

3. Plot time: the structuring or ordering of events from the chronological time of (2) in order to shape the 'here and now' of (1). In the construction of plot time, drama is able to engage in chronological time shifts in the interests of the dramatic present. This is achieved by devices such as the technique of reportage, as discussed above in the Oedipus example, time shifts between acts or scenes, and the use of flash-back sequences.

4. Performance time: The spectator in the theatre is aware that there is a finite period of time for events to take their course, and the sense of limited 'watching' or performance time adds to the tension of 'plot time'. The prologue to *Romeo and Juliet*, for example, functions as an expositional device, not only to establish location, action and character, but also to signal the 'fatal' events about to unfold in 'the two hours' traffic of our stage'. In Ionesco's *Exit the King*, the self-referential indexing of time operates within the dramatic frame: King Bérenger is informed by Marguerite, the elder of his two queens, 'You're going to die in an hour and a half. You're going to die at the end of the show' (1963: 26).

Elam offers a further time dimension which he calls *'historical time'*, i.e. the historical time of the real world as experienced by the spectator in relation to the dramatic world: 'a more or less definite *then* transformed into a fictional *now*'. For further discussion, see Elam 1980: 117–18.)

In a performance context, the spectator's awareness of these temporal planes in relation to the dramatic action may be signified by the deployment of systems of staging in both time and space. A passage of music or the ticking of a clock (temporal) may signify that time has passed. Alternatively, or concurrently, the lowering and raising of the lights (spatial) may be used to achieve the same effect. The verbal weaving of events from chronological time into the 'here and now' of plot time may be visually translated into the space of the stage picture. For example, the past obtrudes on the present action of *Hedda Gabler*, in the form of a portrait of General Gabler – Hedda's dead father – which hangs centre stage throughout. Again, in a production which adopts a Brechtian style, shifts in location or time may be indicated in the stage space via the deployment of slide-projections.

The importance of time to the structuring of dramatic action is well illustrated in the case of plays which seek to undermine the spectator's relation to the dramatic universe via modes of disruption and disorientation. Beckett's techniques of structural disruption (see pp. 67–8) are linked to time games. His dramatic universe of the 'here and now' is populated with characters concerned with the passing of time, or rather its failure to pass. His characters have no sense of chronological and unified autobiographies: neither a structured past giving meaning to the dramatic present, nor a sense of progression towards some future ending, a release from that present. The opening lines of *Endgame*, for example, where Clov declares, 'Finished, it's finished, nearly finished, it must be nearly finished' (12), mirror the progressive weakening of the certainty of closure which underpins the entire drama.

Traditionally, the structuring of dramatic action within a temporal framework does provide us with a 'sense of an ending' which coincides with the end of performance time. Just as a play may open in the middle of a story-line, however, the dramatic plot may have an ending which does not coincide with the close of the narrative line. Furthermore, where openings establish the layers of the past, the closure looks towards the 'future' – immediate and distant. Oedipus is led away to await the decision of the gods regarding his banishment. Where tragedies end in a death which takes place in the 'actual' dramatic world they are usually accompanied by a homily on the new order to follow. At the death of Shakespeare's Macbeth, Malcolm's speech of thanks invites his supporters to attend his coronation. Theseus, as Phaedra expires on stage, proclaims his intention to attend the funeral of his 'ill-starred son' and to see that the latter's good name is restored. Alternatively, in comedies, the convention of a wedding is widely used to signify both an end and a beginning: the end in terms of dramatic plot, a beginning in terms of a new social order. The curtain falls as the festivities and celebrations begin. The events in these examples are not shown but reported as future events, just as, in terms of the openings, past events from the story-line are reported in the dramatic present. They need of course to be only briefly documented; the reader/spectator's interest should be satisfied by the 'sense of an ending', not reawakened by the promise of events they will not 'see'.

TECHNIQUES OF DEFAMILIARISATION

Plays which deviate from this traditional shaping of dramatic plot serve to highlight the rules and conventions governing theatrical construction. Beckett's *Endgame* has no 'ending' as such; rather, the whole play constitutes a winding down (in formal terms) to no logical purpose. Such 'violations of the usual plot structure' (Shklovsky 1965b: 55) were an important part of the formalist analysis of story/plot construction. Shklovsky's analysis of *Tristram Shandy*, cited in the previous chapter, served to show how the combination and transposition of formal properties were essential to the purpose of art: to defamiliarise and de-automatise our perceptions of the world, jaded through habitualisation. Where the formal conventions of the dramatic plot which we have been considering in the previous sections are in some sense 'violated', the devices which govern the shaping of drama are foregrounded and laid bare. This may be illustrated by a final, brief consideration of two further 'openings' which deviate from or violate the conventions previously described in relation to the classic plays, the openings of *The Mother* and *Top Girls*.

Brecht's use of 'alienation' techniques in terms of both dramatic composition and performance style are rooted in the formalist concept of 'making strange', of defamiliarisation. In the opening to *The Mother*, Vlasova's self-referential commentary 'makes strange' the dramatic devices of introduction. Who she is is dealt with in half a sentence: 'a worker's widow and a worker's mother' (6). This 'violates' the convention of major, named characters as a focus of interest in themselves. In this way, Brecht opens with an analysis of oppression in terms of class and gender, rather than in terms of the struggles of an individual, as in the case of Oedipus or Phaedra.

In Churchill's *Top Girls*, our expectations of the dramatic world are subverted by the group of women who gather together in the restaurant. The convention of building a fictional past into the dramatic present is disrupted by Churchill's mixture of female characters drawn from an historical (Pope Joan, Lady Nijo, Isabella Bird) or literary (Patient Griselda) or artistic (Dull Gret) past and the dramatic present (Marlene). These characters from different worlds populate the 'actual' world of the drama. They 'violate' the convention of a fixed, time-bound plane of action.

Commentary on the use of formal properties begins to look reductive if analysis relies only on recognising their use and 'abuse'. Form alone cannot teach us everything about a work of literature, as the structuralists discovered. We need to understand why certain conventions are brought into play or certain formal characteristics are deployed as well as how, and this means moving beyond an analysis of structural *encoding* to the processes of decoding involved in the reading and spectating of drama and theatre. Hence, the violation of formal properties in Brecht's drama is, in the course of reading or decoding, revealed as a political strategy; to show mankind in the process of change, not as fixed individuals as in the concept of Aristotelian drama. Equally, the feminist concerns of Churchill's play underpin the subversive form, to show that patriarchal oppression is not time-bound, but eternal. 'Radical' dramas, like *The Mother*, *Top Girls* and *Endgame*, are the kinds of texts which attract the interest of post-structuralists precisely because of their 'open', violative forms. No spectator will feel comfortable with an opening which splinters the unity between performer and role (*The Mother*), or one which destabilises our expectations of the dramatic universe (*Endgame/Top Girls*).

Because of the way in which such plays disrupt textual expectations and discomfort or unsettle the reader, the space between the writing and the reading in which meaning is produced is made visible. The point has perhaps been most clearly made by Barthes in a later work, *The Pleasure of the Text* (1976 [1973]), where the distinction is drawn between the *plaisir* of the 'closed', comfortable, 'classic' text and the *jouissance* of the 'open', unsettling, 'radical' text. Consider, for example, Kenneth Tynan's comments on seeing the first British production of Beckett's *Waiting for Godot*: 'It forced me to re-examine the rules which have hitherto governed the drama; and, having done so, to pronounce them not elastic enough' (*The Observer*, 7 August 1955). A play which requires the spectator to 're-examine the rules' of drama demands her/his collaboration and active participation in the production of meaning. Such a re-examination challenges the spectator's relation to both the dramatic world and the actual world. It is a process of engagement whereby what is known becomes 'unknown', i.e. the disruptive pleasure of *jouissance*, and which, in consequence, invites a rethinking of the world as it exists.

3

CHARACTER

The Greek term *kharaktēr* signifies three principal, and related, sets of ideas: (1) the literal sense of 'that which is cut in' or 'marked', the 'impress' or 'stamp' on, for example, coins and seals; (2) the metaphorical sense of the 'mark' or 'token impressed on' a person or thing, a 'characteristic' or 'distinctive mark'; (3) a 'likeness', 'image' or 'exact representation' (Liddell and Scott, s.v.). Its transliteration is first used in English to denote 'a personality in a novel or a play' in 1749 (*The Shorter Oxford English Dictionary*, s.v.).

Aristotle, arguing in the *Poetics* that tragedy 'is a representation, not of men, but of action and life, of happiness and unhappiness' and that 'happiness and unhappiness are bound up with action' (Aristotle 1965: 39–40), asserts the primacy of plot over character. We would endorse this argument by suggesting that 'classic' plays such as *Oedipus the King*, *Everyman* and *Phaedra* are most productively read as moral and/or political demonstrations in dramatic form. While human concerns constitute the subject-matter of drama, and while theatre is performed by human agents, so that it follows that 'human beings are both the *content* and the *form* of theater' (Wilson 1976: 97–9), character, in 'classic' drama, is demonstrably a function of action and of the thematic and ideological underpinnings of action. For example, the character of Oedipus is marked by autocratic pride and by religious scepticism. These traits, respectively, identify him with Laius and Jocasta, the parents who should not have conceived him; they are precisely the traits, moreover, to lead him to his predestined fate.

The 'bourgeois' dramatic text, contemporaneous with the realist novel and (in its later phase) with the development of psychology as a system of scientific enquiry, reflects a more conspicuous interest in character *per se*. Strindberg expresses in the preface to *Miss Julie* the view that 'what most interests people today is the psychological process', and acknowledges, in relation to his own practice, a debt to the realist novels of the Goncourt brothers (1976: 99). He states, also, his interest in constructing characters of a complex motivation, 'typical of our times', and indicates his approach in graphic – and idiosyncratic – terms: 'My souls (or characters) are agglomerations of past and present cultures, scraps from books and newspapers, fragments of humanity, torn shreds of once-fine clothing that has become rags, in just the way that a human soul is patched together' (1964: 95). The grounding of characterisation in psychological detail need not detract from the structural and ideological functions of character. In *Miss Julie*, as in *Hedda Gabler*, the characters serve also as representatives of specific class and gender positions; what is laid bare by conflict of character is ideological conflict. Nor does it follow that all 'bourgeois' texts have recourse to a naturalistic psychology. In contradistinction to Ibsen, in whose work the duologue form often calls to mind the analytic encounter, Chekhov preferred to write at the level of the social surface, recording the decline of the landowning classes from an 'objective', external point of view.

Hayman questions the term 'character': 'a dangerous word because it implies a coherence, a consistency and an individuality, which may not be there' (1977: 50). This formulation effectively describes the project, with regard to the construction of character, of the preponderance of 'bourgeois' texts. It also directs us towards an explanation for the development of particular modes of reading (the play-text as novel *manqué*) and spectating (the performance text as animated novel). Furthermore, it usefully reminds us that character, in drama, is constructed wholly within and by means of language, and has no currency beyond the fictional world of the text.

In the 'radical' text, character is re/presented *as* character, i.e. as construct. In *The Mother*, Brecht makes recurrent use of direct address to the audience, breaking down the conventional barriers, spatial and in terms of participation, between actor and spectator. The characters of *Endgame* are aware of their status as characters in a performance process. The dialogue is littered with theatrical metaphor, and Clov at one point ironically surveys the auditorium through a telescope: 'I see . . . a multitude . . . in transports . . . of joy. (*Pause.*) That's what I call a magnifier' (25). Churchill appropriates to the dramatis personae of *Top Girls* two characters, Dull Gret and Patient Griselda, derived respectively from the Brueghel painting, *Dulle Griet*, and from 'The Clerk's Tale' in Chaucer's *The Canterbury Tales*. In each case, the spectator is placed at a critical remove from the action and, in consequence, from the likelihood of reflexive acts of emotional identification with the characters. Hence, a more active mode of spectatorship is placed on offer.

CHARACTER FUNCTIONS

In respect of the application of semiotic methodology to character, an important legacy from the early structuralist and formalist approaches has been the concept of the *functions* of character. This has developed out of the work begun by Propp on the fairy tale, as cited in the historical outline given in Chapter 1. Propp's analysis established a taxonomy of thirty-one functions of the fairy tale. He further added that 'many functions logically join together into certain *spheres*. These spheres *in toto* correspond to their respective performers. They are spheres of action' (1968: 79). He consequently identified seven 'spheres of action' as follows:

1 villain
2 donor (provider)
3 helper
4 princess (a sought-for person) and her father
5 dispatcher
6 hero
7 false hero

In relation to how the characters in a tale carry out these actions, Propp observed that either the character corresponds exactly to the action, or a character changes its function through being involved in several spheres of action, or one sphere of action is carried out by several characters (1968: 79–83). While Propp's narratology is limited to the Russian fairy tale, the notion of linking spheres of action to character offers an important insight into character and the dramatic text.

Amongst those structuralists who have built on the work of Propp is A.J. Greimas (see Hawkes 1977: 87), also influenced by the dramatic theorist Etienne Souriau and his 'calculus' of six roles, apparently worked out independently of Propp (for details, see Greimas 1983: Ch. 10). Through his work on semantics, the structures of meaning, Greimas explored the 'hypothesis of an actantial model . . . proposed as one of the possible principles of organization of the semantic universe' (1983: 199). Like Souriau's 'calculus', Greimas's model proposed six functions and is constituted as shown in Figure 3.1.

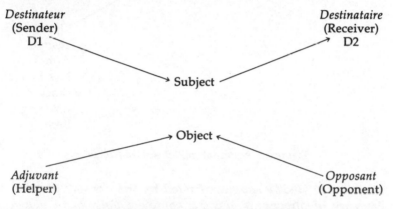

Figure 3.1 Actantial model: Greimas

In this scheme, the sender (D1) is a force or being which acts on the subject thereby initiating the subject's quest for the object in the interests of the receiver (D2), to which end the subject is either helped or opposed. In the case of a love-quest, for example, the subject (hero) seeks the object (heroine) under the influence of Eros (love). Typically, he is helped by confidants or servant-type figures and opposed by parental groupings. In a love-quest model the subject is also the receiver; i.e. motivated by love, the hero acts in his own interests. For illustrative purposes, this model is applied to *Hedda Gabler* in Figure 3.2.

What this actantial model of Ibsen's drama illustrates are the binary, oppositional forces which underpin the tragedy. The

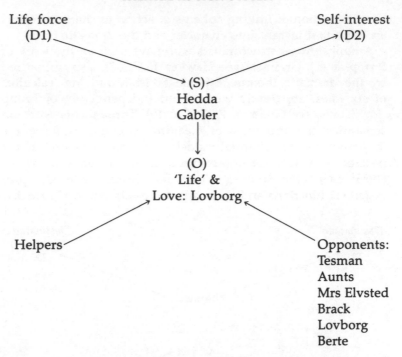

Figure 3.2 Actantial model of *Hedda Gabler*

isolation of Hedda is demonstrated by the densely populated category of opponents and the complete absence of helpers. Given this absence of helpers, the failure of Hedda's quest is signified. If we were to draw up a sequence of diagrams in which the interests of the group of opponents were positioned as subjects, we would conversely find that their quest or object constituted the containment of Hedda in the interests of bourgeois society which they represent. Society is the force which conflicts with the will of the individual and operates as a systematic mode of patriarchal oppression which ultimately realises the destruction of the female subject.

The application of actantial models to dramatic texts provides an illuminating method of identifying the underlying grammar of a play's structure. Developing a sequence of models of different subjects, or looking to the functional changes which occur in respect of the actantial roles within a play can help to understand the underlying structural movement. Ubersfeld

(1978), for example, offers a multiple actantial model of *Phaedra* as shown in Figure 3.3.

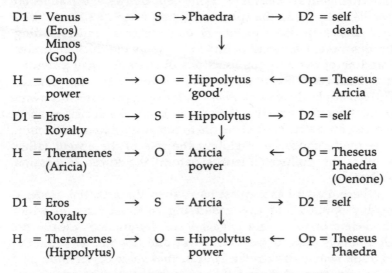

Figure 3.3 Actantial subject models applied to *Phaedra*

Through the application of the multiple model, Ubersfeld is able to offer a way of highlighting the play's underlying structure in order to further our understanding of the dramatic text. She notes that the models show us, for example:

- the parallel love schemes between Hippolytus and Aricia;
- the sphere of action *the desire of Hippolytus* opens the play; the discourse between Theramenes and Hippolytus makes visible the underlying structure;
- Hippolytus is subject once and object twice; Phaedra is subject once and opponent twice;
- Hippolytus as object is blocked in both schemes by his father;
- the love schemes reveal the power/politics of the community hidden beneath the passions of individuals;
- Theseus, the king/father, appears in all three models as an opponent, signifying the failure of all the love schemes. He does not feature as subject; he does not 'will' anything until the close of the drama.

(see Ubersfeld 1978: 97–101)

Ubersfeld works through several examples of actantial models applied to dramatic texts (including an analysis of mirrored movements in *Hamlet* (1978: 93), where Laertes and Hamlet are parallel subjects in the sphere of action *vengeance for the death of a father*), in order to further our structural understanding. Furthermore, Ubersfeld points to the ways in which an understanding of the actantial functions of character may provide a beneficial reference point for those involved in stage practice (1978: 144). In the case of *Phaedra*, for example, directors aware of the tragedy's structural 'grammar' can make decisions about which of the structural elements to foreground in a production. One might choose to highlight the role of the absent father, another the political interests behind the forces of passion, and so on.

Where drama has a quest base, then the actantial model is readily applied and the underlying actantial roles in which characters or forces are engaged are illuminated. Clearly not all drama is constructed in this way and it would be reductive to think wholly in such terms. A further value of attention paid to the function of characters, however, is that it steers us productively away from the negative and misleading approaches encouraged by the method of analysing characters as real people. As Elam states,

> Such an approach, quite evidently, is at the opposite pole from the post-Romantic 'psychologistic' view of character, still current in literary criticism, which sees the dramatis persona as a more or less complex and unified network of psychological and social traits; that is, as a distinct 'personality' rather than as a functive of dramatic structure.
>
> (1980: 131)

Actantial roles are one element in what is the very complex process of character function and signification. Ubersfeld develops her actantial commentary into a subsequent chapter given over entirely to character (see 1978: Ch. 3), where she proceeds to map out a 'grid' for character and to identify the ways in which key functional and semiotic factors are highlighted. We propose to offer an abridged, tabulated summary of her findings (see Table 3.1) in relation to character at the level of text. These include (1) character as lexeme (i.e. as an 'essential unit of vocabulary'), and (2) characters as semiotic ensemble. (In addition to the two categories offered here for consideration, Ubersfeld also covers a third area, that of character and discourse.)

Ubersfeld's study points towards the complexity of character analysis. The cautions, which precede her mapping out of a character-grid and which accompany the explanatory sections, signal the need to consider all of these areas together and to look for relations and interactions: to note, for example, the complex and interconnecting functions of character in relation to actantial or actorial roles. Furthermore, when we study any one character in a play, we need to take account of her/his relations to all of the others and to the many functions and modes of signification. Ultimately, one must then proceed from the textual to the realisation of character on stage, as Ubersfeld's original grid proposes, and add the functional and significatory levels of performance to the equation of character (see Table 3.1).

Table 3.1 Towards a semiotics of character: Ubersfeld

---

1. *Character as lexeme*

Actant:	Character has a 'grammatical' function in dramatic structure and an actantial profile for a character may be established; e.g. Hedda Gabler is the subject of a life/love force, but also has an oppositional function where the interests of Tesman *et al.* are taken as the subject.
Metonymy:	Character functions as a part of a greater whole, or in relation to another or other characters, i.e. a metonymic function; e.g. Berte, the maid, as metonym for the Tesman household.
Metaphor:	Character may function at a metaphorical as well as at a metonymic level; e.g. Tesman as metaphor for patriarchy, oppressive force.
Referent:	Character may be read as a metonymic or metaphoric historico-social referent; e.g. Tesman is a sign which refers to nineteenth-century bourgeois society. (To pursue this point, one needs to move beyond the textual to levels of encoding and decoding in a performance context.)
Connotation:	Denotation of character designates a series of connotative levels; e.g. a character from myth such as Oedipus or Phaedra may, at a connotative level,

Table 3.1 Continued

---

introduce mythical elements above and beyond those actually inscribed in the text. (Again, connotative levels may be exploited or brought out in staging.)

2. *Character as semiotic ensemble*

Actorial function: Where actant constitutes a syntactical unit of narrative, then the *actor* serves as the direct and actual means of carrying out the actantial role; e.g. the actant-opposer in *Hedda Gabler* is lexicalised as *acteur* (e.g. Tesman). Where several actors are involved in the same actorial function then, at one level, characteristics common to all are established; e.g. Tesman, Miss Tesman, Mrs Elvsted, Brack, Lovborg and Berte share the actorial function of actantial opposition, i.e. are all involved in the action of containment. However, they are also marked by characteristics which establish difference, e.g. signs of class, age, gender, status, etc.

Individualisation: The use of characteristics which establish difference may signify an interest in the individual character as in 'bourgeois' theatre. The naming of characters (see pp. 45–6) may signal this.

The role of the individual may also signify entry into a socio-historic context (obvious examples are where an historical figure is taken as a named character in a dramatic fiction).

Collectivisation: The representation of characters may work against an interest in character *per se*. Of importance here are characters who function as a codified role, i.e. are given a pre-determined role to play: e.g. characters in the Commedia dell'Arte, or in melodrama (Lady Audley is the coded role of villain, Robert Audley the hero, etc.); characters who function as socio-cultural abstractions (*à la* Brecht); designation of character via mask (see p.133).

CHARACTER AND FRAME

In his discussion of the construction of the dramatic world, Elam, following Eco, attributes to the spectator the assumption that 'the represented world, unless otherwise indicated, will obey the logical and physical laws' of her/his own world. Hence, there is a marked degree of correspondence between a dramatic world and the characters that inhabit it, and the world of the spectator (1980: 104). On this view, the personified abstractions that comprise the dramatis personae of a medieval morality text such as *Everyman*, or the denaturalised characters of a modernist text such as *Endgame*, work to position the spectator to reflect upon her/his understanding of the external world, rather than break with that world completely.

In relation to the appropriation of historical personages to a dramatic world, Elam enquires as to the extent to which these may be regarded as the 'selfsame' individuals when relocated within a fictional context. He adopts as a single criterion the 'culturally determined *essential properties*' of such figures, arguing, with reference to 'Cleopatra', that any text which 'portrays the heroine in these essential terms will be taken to refer to the historical figure, however much "non-historical" information is added' (1980: 105–6). In the case of a 'Cleopatra' or a 'Napoleon', the name itself is perhaps sufficient to trigger the spectator's broad, cultural knowledge. In the case of less well known figures derived from history, such as the trio who appear in the opening scene of *Top Girls* (Pope Joan, Lady Nijo, Isabella Bird), issues of historical specificity may be subordinate to structural considerations; the project of the scene instanced is to intermix characters drawn from three distinct periods and cultures with characters derived from art and literature.

It follows, from these several examples, that the logic of character definition and representation is not necessarily the logic of the external world, and that a dramatic world which subverts external logic may nonetheless remain accessible to the spectator. Elam cites Pirandello's *Six Characters in Search of an Author*, in which the eponymous sextet enter, from the 'real' world beyond the theatre, to solicit the completion of their dramatic narrative, of which two scenes only have been written (Elam 1980: 109–10). The Characters both enact their scenes and, as a stage audience, watch the scenes enacted by members of a theatre company. The 'real' world, from which the Characters are presumed to originate, is illusory, an off-stage extension of the dramatic world which is 'pointed to' (see also Chapter 4 on Dialogue: Features and Functions). The *trompe-l'oeil* approach to the representation of character serves as a device to engage the spectator in a theatricalised debate on the aesthetics and ethics of performance.

FUNCTION AS CONVENTION

Given that plot, in Greek tragic drama, is constituted through the reordering of material received in the form of mythic narrative, it is apparent that character has attracted to itself a narrative function from the beginnings of theatre, and that a repertoire of conventionalised operations governing the communication of information to the spectator has developed over time. There follows an indication of the primary narrative conventions.

1. *Self-presentation.* A character may introduce herself/himself at the start of the play, as does Oedipus in *Oedipus the King* (lines 7–9), and/or offer supplementary information as appropriate in the course of the action. We noted in Chapter 2, in relation to *The Mother*, that the 'radical' dramatic text is likely to violate such conventions.

2. *Exposition.* Information necessary to the spectator's understanding of the unfolding action, i.e. facts relating to time, place, event and character, is furnished at the outset. It may be offered in the form of a monologue or soliloquy by an unnamed or named character (e.g. the Messenger in *Everyman*, Vlasova in *The Mother*), or in the form of dialogue (e.g. Hippolytus and Theramenes in *Phaedra*).

3. *Choric commentary.* Information necessary to the spectator's understanding of the developing action is furnished on a regular basis. It may be offered by a character or characters within or outside the framework of the narrative, or by a formal chorus with a collective identity (e.g. the Theban Citizens in *Oedipus the King*; the Revolutionary Workers in *The Mother*). In the 'bourgeois' text, both exposition and choric commentary are dialogue-based, in keeping with the naturalistic project.

4. *Character as confidant(e).* A further conventional method of communicating information is the provision of a minor character in whom a more important character may confide. The examples of Celia/Rosalind and Adam/Orlando in *As You Like It*, and Theramenes/Hippolytus, Oenone/Phaedra, and Ismene/Aricia in *Phaedra*, suggest that the confidant(e) figure

44

is a friend or servant of the same sex as the principal character to whom she/he is attached.

5. *Character as foil.* A minor character may also be linked to a principal as a counterpointing device, a means of indexing similarity (e.g. Ania/Varia in *The Cherry Orchard*) or difference (e.g. Mrs Elvsted/Hedda in *Hedda Gabler*). (See Wilson 1976: 96, for a useful analogy with painting.)

6. *Deus ex machina* ('god from the machine'). In the Greek theatre, a crane-like device (*mekane*) was employed to hoist a god on the roof of the stage-building, in order that the complexities of the action might be resolved at the conclusion of the play. A comparable function is served by Rosalind, now again attired in woman's clothing, in *As You Like It*, V.4.

7. *Silent characters.* Narrative information may be conveyed purely in visual terms: *Oedipus the King* opens with a tableau vivant, an image of supplication, Act III of *The Cherry Orchard* with a travesty of a formal ball. In both cases, there is a subsequent verbal commentary upon the action. Conversely, Clov's establishing mime in *Endgame* remains unglossed and enigmatic.

8. *Character names.* To assert that names signify is to state no more than the obvious. It may, however, be demonstrated that the names of dramatis personae signify in a number of ways that bear on the informational function of character. The name Oedipus designates 'Swellfoot', a reference to the pinioned, foundling child. The text of *Oedipus the King* plays continually on the name; for example, with a minimal shift in stress, the Greek may be pronounced *Oi-dipous*, 'Ah! Two-Foot', the solution to the sphinx's riddle (Ferguson 1972: 181–2). The term rendered as 'King', *turannos*, conveys the sense of 'absolute ruler', 'autocrat'. The names of the personified abstractions in *Everyman* index a symbolic level of operation; those of le Beau and Sir Oliver Martext in *As You Like It*, courtier and rural cleric respectively, exert a satirical function. The reader/spectator is aware of both first name and surname in all but two cases with regard to the dramatis personae of *Hedda Gabler*: Brack, the judge, is always addressed or referred to in formal terms, in deference to his position; Berte, the Tesmans' servant, a non-position, is addressed by her first name only. In *The Mother*, minor characters are regularly named in terms of occupation and, by extension, class position or allegiance (e.g. Policeman,

Factory Porter, Butcher, Strikebreaker). In *Endgame*, the names of the characters constitute a further enigma.

ACTOR/CHARACTER

The project of differentiating between the 'character' (i.e. the constructed psychology) and the functions (structural, ideological, theatrical and so on) of character in drama must ultimately take account of the actor. Within the theatrical context, the actor serves as the agent whereby character is mediated to the spectator. While we would stress that performance style and stage–spectator relations are culturally and historically specific, in each period of theatre history it is the actor who constitutes, in her/his person, the primary channel whereby character is communicated. If the function of the actor is on occasion assumed by an inanimate 'agent', such as a puppet (Honzl 1976: 75) or the machines designed by Oskar Schlemmer (von Maur 1982: 213–15), it is not materially changed.

In the earlier, open-air theatres, the actor-in-role functioned as a sign of the personated character. Once theatre moved indoors (for entrepreneurial purposes, at the close of the sixteenth century), the distinction between the real and the role was progressively blurred. As the actor worked to identify herself/himself with the character, so the spectator was repositioned to engage in comparable acts of identification. In the modern period, a space has again been opened up between actor and role. The spectator is now positioned, by the conjunction of 'radical' text and anti-illusionistic performance aesthetic, at a critical remove from the dramatic fiction. We may label the three performance modes outlined here in relation to the respective textual forms:

Textual form	*Performance mode*
1. Classic text	Conventionalised representation
2. Bourgeois text	Analogical representation
3. Radical text	Deconstructive representation

We shall pursue these issues in further detail in Chapter 5. It may be noted in passing, however, that the distinction between modes two and three has been historically reinforced at the level of actor training. Hence, for Stanislavsky the actor is to be regarded as an artist who may, by a process of instruction and self-interrogation, for the duration of a performance 'become' the character she/he plays. The contrast with the politicised, Brechtian actor is stark:

Stanislavskian	Brechtian
Actor as artist	Actor as worker
Actor as character	Actor as narrator
Internalisation	Externalisation
Psychology	Social context
Identification	Deconstruction
Ideological affirmation	Ideological contestation

As offered to the spectator by the actor-in-role, character involves three distinct levels of operation. The actor plays a character that functions (1) as a psychological construct, (2) as a thematic symbol and/or ideological 'key', and (3) as a mirror-image of the individual spectator. It will be apparent that these categories are not mutually exclusive, that they are offered as generalisations, and that they may well operate simultaneously. The character of Oedipus is drawn consistently if in outline terms; it may be read as a function of the thematic equation between human aspiration and divine retribution, and in the context of a specific nexus of political and religious values. It may, on this basis, be read as an *exemplum*. The individual spectator inhabited the same metaphysical universe as the blighted Oedipus, and was subject equally to its laws. It might be argued, further, that Oedipus stands for the collective spectatorship, and thus for the city of Athens, now a prideful and imperialistic power, already visited by plague, embroiled in a panhellenic war which was ultimately to break her.

The actor-in-role is faced with the probability of role-play at the level of *character*. Given the broad applicability of the world-stage metaphor, the actor will play a character that is more likely than not to assume a role or roles within the course of the action. Again, three levels are involved.

1 The actor plays a character that plays a role 'reflexively', i.e. as a theatricalised extension of 'social acting'. In *Lady Audley's Secret*, Lady Audley, having 'married for wealth' (245), sustains the role of devoted and supportive wife.

2 The actor plays a character that assumes a second identity, by the adoption of disguise or by some other means. In *As You Like It*, the banished Rosalind protects herself in exile by disguising herself as a young man, Ganymede.

3 The actor plays a character who participates in a formal, second-level enactment, a play or masque within the play. *The Murder of Gonzago*, the play within *Hamlet*, and the double masque in *The Revenger's Tragedy*, interludes devised respectively to detect and to enact murder, serve as cases in point.

'Inner' acting draws attention to its own status as acting, deconstructing the performance process and revealing the actor behind the character. It is a highly self-referential mode of performance, and has a particular currency in relation to the 'radical' text. In Apollinaire's *The Breasts of Tiresias*, for example, the sex-change of Thérèse is indexed by the 'loss' of her breasts, the marks of her femininity here. In the form of balloons, they detach themselves and float away. In Whiteside's terms, the balloons 'now refer to themselves as theatrical props, as self-referring artifacts in the very process of self-reference, floating between androgyny and their own autonomy' (1988: 35).

CHARACTER AND PSYCHOLOGY

We have noted, with reference to Strindberg, that the 'bourgeois' text is to a significant degree marked by an approach to character representation based in the emergent science of psychology. The critical establishment, responding to this new development with an enthusiastic (if often less than informed) interest, extended the scope of psychologically inflected enquiry to the dramatic literature of the earlier periods. Work such as A.C. Bradley's *Shakespearean Tragedy* (1961 [1904]), which treated the texts virtually as case histories of 'real' people, has proved influential to the extent that character has been perceived as an object of study in its own right, rather than as a structural and thematic device. The problem is compounded by practices of reading which blur the distinctions between novel and play-text, failing to recognise that the dramatist is in general concerned to offer information on character sufficient to enable the reader/spectator to make sense of the *action* at any given point. Dramatic characters have no existence beyond their scenes, and the dramatist has little cause to emulate the depth and detail of characterisation typical of the nineteenth-century realist novel.

One branch of psychology, psychoanalysis, has exerted a particular influence upon literary and dramatic criticism. On the one hand, the psychoanalyst has had recourse to the literary or dramatic text in order to corroborate or to generalise clinical observation, or to remark a parallel to clinical practice. On the other hand, the textual critic has become increasingly engaged by the connections to be drawn between psychoanalytic theory and theories of literature and the arts.

In the 1916 article 'Some Character-Types met with in Psychoanalytic Work', Freud refers to Ibsen as a dramatist who 'loves to pursue problems of psychological responsibility with unrelenting rigour' (1985: 308), before proceeding to an analysis of the character of Rebecca West in Ibsen's *Rosmersholm*. Freud's project here is to adduce the case of Rebecca as a parallel to the Oedipal trajectory of the male child, to demonstrate an incestuous relationship with her 'father' and an unconscious desire to replay this, with a concomitant ousting of a 'mother', in relation to the father-figure of Rosmer. While this example offers an insight into the psychoanalyst's use of a dramatic text, it also highlights the recurrent danger of misreadings that, on occasion, seem to border on the wilful. Dr West is Rebecca's stepfather, not her father, and the assertion of a sexual relationship with him is made on one occasion only and then by a hostile witness.

Freud repeatedly noted that many of his clinical observations and theoretical positions had been anticipated by creative writers. Georges Devereux, in the 1970 article 'The Psychotherapy Scene in Euripides' *Bacchae*', seeks to demonstrate, by means of a 'purely psychiatric analysis', the clinical plausibility of the scene in which Cadmus relieves Agave of the condition of Dionysiac possession. He concludes that the scene is 'clinically flawless and persuasive', that it would stand comparison with 'any modern summary' of a psychotherapeutic treatment written by a professional practitioner, and that the dramatist's observation and description of both the psychological illness and the curative process is informed and accurate (1970: 47–8).

With regard to psychoanalytically oriented literary criticism, Terry Eagleton has suggested four levels of application: 'It can attend to the *author* of the work; to the work's *contents*; to its *formal construction*; or to the *reader.'* He notes that criticism in the field has commonly addressed the first two topics, with limited results (1983: 179). The psychoanalysis of the author is a speculative practice analogous to the pursuit of intentionality. An extreme example, founded on the assumption that contrasting characters are to be read as projections of unresolved authorial contradictions, is able to conclude that 'Shakespeare was both Othello and Iago' (Griffiths 1982: 58)! Approaches to content tend to deal with the unconscious motivation of character or with the symbolic signification of objects, and have tended towards the reductive or naive. The current post-structuralist interest in the broader application of psychoanalytic theory is, however, producing a corpus of informed and sober critical work (see, e.g., Donald 1983, Wright 1984, Burgin *et al.* 1986, Rimmon-Kenan 1987, Feldstein and Sussman 1990), which places on offer more productive methodologies for the analysis of the dramatic text *per se* and for the interrogation of the processes of reading and spectating.

4

DIALOGUE

Given that structuralist and semiotic approaches to the dramatic text have established character as fictions constructed through language, and called into question psychologising modes of enquiry which efface the distinction between dramatic construct and real person, as the previous chapter showed, it follows that such approaches should pay detailed attention to the dialogue modes through which the dramatic fiction is created. A key aim of semioticians in relation to the dramatic text is to understand and identify the main characteristics of dramatic discourse.

In order to work on the semiotics of dialogue, an initial distinction may be usefully made between the main body of dramatic text and the text containing stage directions. This distinction was formulated by Roman Ingarden as *Haupttext* and *Nebentext* (Ingarden 1973: 208). This chapter and the following are devoted respectively to these two 'texts'. Some cross-referencing is required, notably in relation to those instructions whose function it is to direct speech.

Understanding the processes of the linguistic sign-system is a necessary adjunct to furthering our analysis of how a dramatic text operates. At the same time, language studies which adopt a linguistic approach may prove heavily jargon-laden and difficult to decipher, so care needs to be taken to avoid this. Furthermore, an additional risk arises if the explanations of language usage are prioritised at the expense of the dramatic analysis (see Burton 1980). Despite such risks, this route of investigation is entirely preferable and significantly more profitable than the 'traditional' approaches to drama which remain essentially descriptive (see, e.g., Hayman 1977; Griffiths 1982),

51

failing as they do to proceed beyond an identification of the effects of language to an analysis of *how* such effects are achieved. We will argue that, used judiciously, a semiotic analysis of language can show us how such effects are created and prove productive, systematic and informative as opposed to reductive, random or descriptive.

We propose to adopt a systematic approach to dialogue analysis, with the aim of identifying the dominant characteristics and functions of the ways in which dialogue is used to structure dramatic discourse, and to use our contextualising generic framework based on the three historical phases of drama.

DIALOGUE: FEATURES AND FUNCTIONS

It is generally the role of dialogue in dramatic texts to establish character, space and action. In its most common form, dialogue is structured as a turn-taking system. One character addresses another who listens and then replies, in turn becoming the speaker. The interactive duality of the speaker–listener role is a basic mode of dramatic dialogue, and one which we can trace back to the line-for-line exchanges of Greek tragedy (*stichomythia*), which constitute a fundamental form for actor–actor sequences and for those in which the chorus-leader operates as a fourth actor (e.g. in *Oedipus the King*: 'OEDIPUS: But you know more than I,/you should, you've seen the man before. LEADER: I know him definitely. One of Laius' men,/ a trusty shepherd, if there ever was one': 225). Its mode is essentially deictic. As Elam states, 'What allows the dialogue to create an interpersonal dialectic . . . within the time and location of discourse is the *deixis*' (1980: 139). *Deixis*, literally 'pointing', is the means by which the I–You exchanges are constructed; personal and demonstrative pronouns ('I', 'You', 'this', 'that', etc.) and 'deictic adverbials' ('here', 'now', etc.) are used by the speakers to point to themselves, to others and to their context, in the process of communication (1980: 72–3). In short, 'it is important now to note that the drama consists first and foremost precisely in this, an *I* addressing a *you here* and *now*' (ibid.: 139). It is through the deictic interchange that the dramatic world achieves its three-dimensionality; that the bare bones are fleshed out. The speaker-listeners 'point' not only to the 'actual' or 'mimetic' (i.e. visibly represented) world, but to unseen characters, events or spaces, making them part of the fictional universe through reference. (For a more detailed discussion of mimetic and 'diegetic' spaces, see Issacharoff: 1981.)

Whilst the use of *deixis* establishes the speakers and their space, the sequencing of utterances is also central to the action. Traditionally, action in drama has only been considered in terms of external action, but semioticians have tried to show how the use of language also constitutes a form of action. The speech-act theory, developed by the philosophers of language (Austin, Grice, Searle *et al.*), has provided the foundation for this. A detailed analysis of the development and refinement of this theory is beyond the scope and range of the present book, but a brief indication of its applicability to the dramatic text is in order. The three levels of speech as action which need concern us here are the locutionary (uttering a sentence that makes sense), the illocutionary (the act performed in speaking the sentence, e.g. making a request or promise, issuing a command) and the perlocutionary (the effect on the addressee through what is said, e.g. the act of persuading). Not all utterances are met with the called-for action-response, and investigating the conditions for a speech act to be *felicitous*, i.e. to result in a successful uptake, further informs the work of language philosophers (see Searle 1969).

Our investigations into dialogue therefore begin with an analysis of how the linguistic sign-system of the dramatic text actively points to the characters and world of the dramatic universe in the 'here and now' and functions as the means of creating action through speech. To illustrate these fundamental points, let us consider them in relation to the following extract from *Hedda Gabler*, where Hedda makes her first appearance in the play:

MISS TESMAN (*going up to* HEDDA). Good morning, Hedda dear! A very good morning to you!

HEDDA (*holding out her hand*). Good morning, my dear Miss Tesman. What an early visit! It was kind of you.

MISS TESMAN (*seeming a little taken aback*). Well, has the bride slept well in her new home?

HEDDA. Oh yes, thank you. Tolerably.

TESMAN. Tolerably! I like that, Hedda! You were sleeping like a
log when I got up.

HEDDA. Fortunately. In any case, one has to get used to anything
new, Miss Tesman. By degrees. (*Looking to the left.*) Oh!
The maid has gone and opened the veranda door! There's
a perfect flood of sunlight coming in.

MISS TESMAN (*going towards the door*). Well, we'll shut it, then.

HEDDA. Oh no, don't do that, please. (*To* TESMAN.) Just draw the
blinds, my dear, will you? That gives a softer light.

TESMAN (*at the door*). Yes, yes. All right. There you are, Hedda.
Now you've got shade *and* fresh air.

HEDDA. Yes, we certainly need fresh air in here. All these
precious flowers! But – won't you sit down, Miss Tesman?

MISS TESMAN. No, thank you very much. Now I know everything
is going on all right here – thank goodness! – I must see
about getting home again. Poor dear, she finds the time
very long, lying there.

TESMAN. Give her my love and my best wishes, won't you? And
tell her I'll come over and see her later on today.

(272–3)

The deictic nature of the I–You exchanges between the three
characters is immediately apparent, as is the 'here and now'
spatial context. Because it is the 'here and now' conditions
of the space which constitute the main topic of conversation,
they are frequently 'pointed' to in the dialogue, and it is Hedda,
who is taking stock of her new home (space), who does most
of the 'pointing'; 'fresh air in *here*'/'*these* flowers', etc. If we
further consider the dialogue in relation to the notion of speech
as action, Hedda's dominance – both spatial and social –
becomes apparent. The initial greeting between Miss Tesman
and Hedda is a prime example. The warmth and familiarity of
Miss Tesman's greeting (confirmed by the 'movement towards'
stage direction) does not elicit the called-for response. Hedda
observes the rule of polite behaviour by making an appropriate
reply, but accompanies this with a movement away ('*holding out*

her hand') and a further utterance, 'What an early visit! It was kind of you', where clearly what is said is not what is meant. (See Searle on Wittgenstein 1971: 46.) Hedda's discontent with her 'space' and with those in it continues to manifest itself in a series of speech acts where utterance and meaning diverge. 'There's a perfect flood of sunlight coming in', appears at one level to be a simple utterance not demanding a response. However, it exerts an illocutionary force, being a request for something to be done and further produces a perlocutionary effect: Miss Tesman goes to close the veranda door. Hedda stops her and requests, or rather indirectly commands, her husband to 'draw the blinds'. Her dominance or superior status is therefore constructed through the conversation. (On status, see Burton 1980: 70.) The illocutionary force of her requests, whether direct or indirect, place her in a position of authority. Hence, by the time Hedda asks if Miss Tesman would like a seat, the latter has been made too uncomfortable and unwelcome in the space for her to accept. Instead she announces her intention of leaving to join an unseen character (her sister) in an unseen diegetic space (their home), thereby demonstrating dialogue's ability to extend the boundaries of the fictional universe.

A reading of this extract in the traditions of literary-critical practice would probably tell us in broad terms how Hedda is presented as the dominant character and locate her command of the scene in the way in which Tesman and his sister are subservient to her wishes. The advantage of a reading which takes account of the dramatic discourse along the lines proposed above is that, in addition, it will productively lead us towards an understanding of exactly *how* this overall effect is achieved.

VERSE AND PROSE

While examining specific characteristics of dramatic discourse, we can also align such features and functions with the general modes or registers in which dialogue takes its form, and here generic considerations may be significant. In the sample of dialogue from *Hedda Gabler*, the turn-taking process of character–character, speaker–listener interaction took the form of 'ordinary' speech, even though, as analysis shows, this is a highly structured and artificial process. It is generally the case that prose dialogue seeks to replicate 'ordinary' language. Verse dialogue, on the other hand, is characterised by the presence of 'artistic' language demonstrating a specialised usage: metaphor, simile, rhyme and so on. (The artistic/ordinary distinction is taken from Todorov 1973.) While dramatic discourse may appropriate either of these two modes, the choice of register has a significant impact on the processes of meaning-production.

In terms of generic evolution, verse has traditionally been associated with tragedy and prose with comedy. Just as theoretical notions of an 'ideal' form have affected dramatic structures, so modes of dramatic expression have also been linked to notions of an appropriate register. Tragedy, in its classical form, constructs a dramatic world populated by royal households, whose dialogue must be as dignified and as lofty as their status. Aristotle, with reference to tragic diction, noted that 'The clearest diction is that which consists of words in everyday use, but this is commonplace . . . a diction abounding in unfamiliar usages has dignity, and is raised above the everyday level' (1965: 62–3). It is not assumed that kings and queens speak in verse, but that this is a convention of dialogue form which signifies the dramatic world of tragic heroines/heroes. (Note that, when wishing to designate language in its pure form, we still speak of 'the Queen's English'.) Conversely, the low-life world of comedy is more appropriately expressed through an 'everyday' language signifying the 'commonplace'. Even those comedies in the classic tradition which operate in verse, or in a mixed mode of verse and prose (Aristophanes, Plautus, Molière *et al.*), invite the 'commonplace' by permitting the use of dialect or colloquial expression. Or verse is used as a means to parody the tragic (as opposed to ennobling the comic).

We may further consider the appropriateness of dialogue forms in tragedy and comedy in terms of their ideological discourse. To be brief, the tragic discourse is based on philosophical dialogues of right and wrong. In terms of thematic or ideological continuity, it aims to provide universal 'truths' in order to give 'meaning' to life. These will be culture-specific and include, for example, the reaffirmation of the hierarchical laws of the gods and mankind in Greek tragedy, or the 'hidden gods' and unlawful passions in Racinian tragedy. This contrasts with comedy, where discourse is essentially social and aims, through play, to explode the systems of order through which society seeks to give itself structure and meaning. In comedy social behaviour is under scrutiny; in tragedy moral dilemmas are debated. This fundamental difference, in conjunction with notions of appropriate registers, has a significant impact on the meaning-creating processes of dialogue. This we can investigate further by applying our general deductions to specific examples of tragedy and comedy from a 'classic' period.

DIALOGUE AND THE 'CLASSICS'

Chapter 2 identified the 'graded' and graphic form of classical tragedy, demonstrating the way in which the action of the plot carries the tragic victims to their fates. Clearly, one fundamental function of the dialogue is to further this external action, and language, as we subsequently observed, is capable of generating action. Furthermore, the significance of an event may lie not in the event itself, but in what *is said* about it. When Macbeth is finally killed by Macduff, it is not his death itself which is of significance, but the 'truths' which are spoken in consequence. The dialogue must therefore be structured in such a way as to draw our attention to its content. Consider the words spoken by the dying Phaedra in the final scene of the tragedy:

Each moment's precious. Listen. It was I,
Theseus, who on your virtuous, filial son
Made bold to cast a lewd, incestuous eye.
Heaven in my heart lit an ill-omened fire.
Detestable Oenone did the rest.
She feared your son, knowing my frenzy, might
Reveal a guilty passion he abhorred.
The wretch, exploiting my enfeebled state,
Rushed to denounce Hippolytus to you.
She has exacted justice on herself
And found beneath the waves too mild a death.
But first I wished to clear my victim's name.
I wished, revealing my remorse to you,
To choose a slower road down to the dead.
I have instilled into my burning veins
A poison that Medea brought to Greece.
Already it has reached my heart and spread
A strange chill through my body. Even now

Only as through a cloud I see the bright
Heaven and the husband whom I still defile.
But death, robbing my eyes of light, will give
Back to the sun its tarnished purity.

(213–14)

Although these words are addressed to her husband, they assume the form of a speech. The length of the address contravenes the traditional turn-taking sequence of 'spoken' dialogue. It does not require an interaction or response, but functions as a self-contained statement which constitutes a public admission of guilt.

What is represented here is dialogue composed in 'artistic' language. Erike Fischer-Lichte has usefully identified the two 'extreme forms of literary dramatic dialogue' as follows: 'The first is characterized by a predominance of linguistic features that are common in written language and the second by the prevailing use of such features that denote spoken language' (1984: 139). As an example of the first form, the lyric dramas of the Romantics or neo-Romantics are cited, and the second is illustrated with reference to the naturalistic drama. It is, however, stressed that these are not mutually exclusive forms, and that what occurs generally in drama is a combination of the two. *Phaedra* is more firmly aligned with the first category. The linguistic signs of the dialogue are characterised by the features of 'artistic' as opposed to 'ordinary' or spoken language, and operate as signifiers of the status of the characters in the world of tragedy. The dialogue is replete with the tragic vocabulary of Racinian drama. The binary images of light and darkness, purity and impurity, are typical of the play's specialised poetic use of language (reinforced in the original French by the use of the classical alexandrine verse structure). When this type of dialogue is performed, it is delivered, as Fischer-Lichte states, 'as if it were an oral communication' (1984: 139). It belongs, in performance terms, to the tradition which prioritises language over acting (ibid.: 154). In such a tradition, it is the function of the 'nonverbal signs' to support the 'linguistic signs' (ibid.: 158). Though relatively little is known about the performance conditions of French classical tragedy, it is thought that the acting style relied on minimal movement by the actors (a restriction reinforced by the wearing of high-heeled boots),

58

and that the staging was simple in its representation of the abstract *palais à volonté*. In short, the linguistic sign-system is prioritised in terms of its own 'artistic' mode and is hierarchised in theatrical terms in relation to the other sign-systems operating in a performance context. The dominance of the linguistic sign-system therefore ensures the reader/spectator's focus on *what* is said, and on the philosophical 'truths' embodied by the dialogue.

In comedy, the ideological discourse is social rather than philosophical. Human behaviour is subject to comic scrutiny and is held up to ridicule for our delight and entertainment, rather than offered for contemplation. Hence, where tragedy, in its 'classic' form, has recourse to long and 'artistic' speeches in which it is supposed that the reader/spectator is the primary listener as opposed to another character (as in the Phaedra/Theseus 'dialogue'), comedy offers greater dialogic, social interaction between characters. For this reason alone, one would expect to find a linguistic sign-system which belongs more firmly to Fischer-Lichte's second type of 'literary dramatic dialogue'; where 'ordinary' language is the dominant mode, but where the linguistic sign is less significant in the hierarchy of sign-systems and where meaning is therefore generated not through the *Haupttext* alone, but through recourse to the *Nebentext* (i.e. to interpret actions, gestures and so on). This is certainly true of comedies which rely heavily on farcical action. An Edwardian pantomime script, for instance, consists predominantly of *Nebentext* to mark out the action, and the dialogue of the *Haupttext* is positively minimal.

As You Like It offers a combination of both types of dialogue, is structured in verse and prose, and demonstrates a constant crossing of linguistic sign-systems characterised by the 'written' and the 'spoken'. It is prose, however, which dominates and 'for the most part the effect of the prose in this play is one of informality, of people talking rather than of actors declaiming' (Shakespeare 1975: xx). In the main, verse is reserved for the occasional moments when gravity touches the comedy and the 'artistic' features of verse are used to foreground the serious note. For example, Duke Frederick's banishment of Rosalind in I.3 is decreed in verse, because it carries the threat of death: 'If you outstay the time, upon mine honour,/And in the greatness of my word you die' (line 26). The illocutionary force of the promise of death has the perlocutionary effect of driving the protagonists into the Forest of Arden. (On the danger and power of words, see Elam 1988: 39–40.)

The pastoral comedy of the court in exile relies on furthering misunderstanding. This contrasts with the tragic world, where the proclamation of a philosophical 'truth' is read as an act of sincerity. When Phaedra regrets and laments over her actions at the moment of her death, it is assumed she is sincere. Tragic heroes and heroines may be self-deceivers (Oedipus, Phaedra) or deceived by others (Othello), but the moral 'truths' they realise through the course of their actions are assumed to *be* truths, not lies. Sincerity is one of the conditions identified by Searle (1969) for the successful or felicitous performance of a speech act. Where Elam argues for the abuse of these conditions in speech acts in drama (Iago/Othello being a prime example, 1980: 163), we would argue that such an abuse is in greater evidence in comedy than tragedy.

Comedy thrives on lies and deceptions and pursues ambiguity rather than clarifying meaning. Its action frequently operates through deceit and disguise, both in terms of the external action and through language itself. In a serious moment, as in the Duke's promise of death, there is no doubting that what is said is what is meant; the meaning of utterance is fixed and unambiguous. But in comic mood, language is licensed for play. It is the means through which play is constructed and at the same time is an object of play in itself. Comedies in the classical tradition frequently separate the two. To take Northrop Frye's commentary on the recurrent, formulaic patterns of structure and character for comedy (1971: 163–86): play through action (disguise, mistaken identity, *et al.*) is often the dominant mode for the struggles between the *eiron* (hero) and *alazon* (blocking character) which polarise the action, and play through language operates as a dominant mode for the buffoon-type characters who create the comic mood which punctuates the action. Sometimes the two coincide, as in the complications of the Arden disguises, and the verbal wit of the mock-wooing. In such scenes, the action is moved on (Rosalind and Orlando make 'promises' to meet) and the verbal sparring is an occasion for the comic mood of 'holiday humour'. The complications arising from the many disguises are mirrored in the disguises of the dramatic discourse *per se*:

ROS. Am not I your Rosalind?

ORL. I take some joy to say you are, because I would be talking of her.

ROS. Well, in her person, I say I will not have you.

ORL. Then in mine own person, I die.

(97–8)

Here, the use of *deixis* is a direct source of comic irony. Rosalind's self-referential 'I' points to a fictional 'I' which is in fact the real 'I', known to the audience but not to Orlando. Because we know that the 'I' who is Rosalind would not refuse Orlando, his perlocutionary response to this threat – 'I die' – is also invalidated. The act of generating action through speaking is therefore turned upside down into the act of speaking of actions which will go no further than words. The deictic use of the 'I' licensed for comic play relies on furthering ambiguity of identity and self-referentiality. When the 'I' is 'fixed', and refers unreservedly to the 'I' who speaks, then conditions of sincerity and felicitous uptake are restored. (On the 'I' in discourse and the 'I' who speaks, see the section on 'radical' drama, p. 69.) When Orlando's brother Oliver appears in the forest in Act IV, for example, Rosalind and Celia question him to establish his identity:

CELIA. Are you his brother?

ROS.   Was't you he rescu'd?

CELIA. Was't you that did so oft contrive to kill him?

OLIVER. 'Twas I. But 'tis not I. I do not shame
    To tell you what I was, since my conversion
    So sweetly tastes, being the thing I am.

(109)

Oliver's 'I', which claims a new identity, parallels the comic use of changing identities, but is a sincere and serious revelation of selfhood, signified by the religious overtones of 'conversion' and the use of blank verse. The point is reinforced through the contrasting restoration of the comic mood (heralded by the return to prose), and by Rosalind's 'counterfeiting' of gender role and identity.

DIALOGUE IN 'BOURGEOIS' TRAGEDY AND COMEDY

Where the use of verse and prose registers has generic associations in a 'classic' age of drama, by the second half of the nineteenth century, the 'bourgeois' century, the use of verse-dialogue (blank or rhymed) is no longer a dominant mode in tragedy, and both genres draw mainly on 'spoken' as opposed to 'artistic' language. In very crude terms, this reflects a generic shift in which tragedy is 'downgraded' and comedy 'upgraded', and in which the worlds of royalty and low life are replaced by one social milieu which lies somewhere in between the two. As the concerns of the emergent middle classes gradually came to dominate the century, so drama moved increasingly towards a mimetic and mundane realisation of the bourgeois values which conditioned the theatres, plays, players and spectators of the period.

As drama and 'life' in some sense moved closer together, so dramatic dialogue moved closer to 'everyday' speech. Whether a play was comic or tragic, it needed to create the impression of a world inhabited by 'real' people holding 'everyday' conversations to recreate the social milieu which was familiar to and experienced by its middle-class audiences. In the pursuit of 'realism' such conversations were staged over tea-cups, across ballrooms or around dinner tables, and dramatic dialogue, as a consequence, mirrored the polite formulations and codes of etiquette which informed these rules of social behaviour.

In Oscar Wilde's comedy *The Importance of Being Earnest*, the characters are seen in a variety of social-eating contexts, fashionable among the titled society figures of late Victorian society from whom the middle classes took their cue:

CECILY. May I offer you some tea, Miss Fairfax?

GWENDOLEN (*with elaborate politeness*). Thank you. (*Aside.*) Detestable girl. But I require tea!

CECILY (*sweetly*). Sugar?

GWENDOLEN (*superciliously*). No, thank you. Sugar is not fashionable any more.

(CECILY *looks angrily at her, takes up the tongs and puts four lumps of sugar into the cup.*)

CECILY (*severely*). Cake or bread and butter?

GWENDOLEN (*in a bored manner*). Bread and butter, please. Cake is rarely seen at the best houses nowadays.

CECILY (*cuts a very large slice of cake, and puts it on the tray*). Hand that to Miss Fairfax.

(1988: 265)

In this representational sequence from the play's second act, Cecily (as hostess) puts a series of 'polite' questions to Gwendolen in accordance with the dictates of social etiquette. The question form is designed to elicit a 'yes/no' type of response, but Gwendolen, in each instance, elaborates and rationalises her response into an insult which attacks Cecily's society-hostess role. Cecily retaliates by following her questions with an action which constitutes a reciprocal insult. The *Nebentext* is significant in so far as it helps to 'fix' the tone and direct the stage action. The female battle over the tea-cups (paralleled subsequently by the male duelling over the muffins and tea-cakes) is therefore built on a dialogue pattern of 'spoken' language which takes the form of: Question + Attack (Verbal)/Answer + Attack (Verbal)/Attack (Action). The pattern is appropriate to character: Gwendolen, the London lady, has command of the 'spoken' word appropriate to her society circles, Cecily, the country girl, resorts to childlike actions to express her displeasure.

Deception and disguise are as integral to Wilde's comedy as they are to *As You Like It*. The invention of Bunbury and the Bunbury vocabulary point to the self-generating capacity of language. To 'deceive in the quest of pleasure', i.e. to 'Bunbury', is both the structural root of the comedy and a sign of language licensed for play. The linguistic sign-system is used in such a way as to lay bare its essentially arbitrary and deceptive nature, in order pleasurably to unmask the 'lies' of an age where social identities are only as 'real' as the language that creates them.

An examination of how dominant features of dramatic discourse are used in the dialogue of a particular play may reveal generic indicators (e.g. subversion of deictic rules in the comedy of *As You Like It*) or linguistic signs of ideological content (e.g. speech-act greetings signifying social conflict in *Hedda Gabler*). In Chekhov's *The Cherry Orchard*, the linguistic sign-system is the key to the play's meditation on a displaced sector of society; the displacement of the aristocracy by a new 'class' of freed serfs. The inability of the former group to move with the changing times is reflected in a dramatic discourse whose features resist the common pattern of action through words:

LIUBOV ANDRYEEVNA. How does it go now? Let me think. . . . I pot the red. . . . I go off into the middle pocket!

GAYEV. I pot into the corner pocket! . . . Years ago you and I slept in this room, little brother and sister together; and now I'm fifty-one, strange as it may seem.

LOPAHIN. Yes, time flies.

GAYEV. What?

LOPAHIN. Time flies, I say.

GAYEV. This place smells of patchouli . . .

(340–1)

In this sequence, as the characters assemble to take coffee together, resistance is signified in Gayev's refusal to enter into an appropriate, engaged response with Lopahin. A reply, such as 'Does it?', to Lopahin's 'time flies' would have created the potential for moving the conversation forwards into subsequent explanations of change. Instead, the inappropriate 'What?' invites repetition and a refusal to engage in the usual forward-moving, speaker–listener/listener–speaker, turn-taking system. Lopahin's illocutionary statement is left hanging and is not pursued as a topic of conversation. Instead, Gayev's discourse is marked by a preoccupation with the past. The dominance of spatial indicators, 'this room', 'this place' and the 'double pointing' to 'you and I'/'brother and sister', signal an attempt to reaffirm a sense of location and identity which are under threat in the 'here and now' of the dramatic present. Preoccupation with space signifies a resistance to the temporal; the room is still known as the nursery, a spatial metaphor for the golden age of childhood and resistance to time passing.

The play's dialogue is predominantly constructed out of a society in conversation, where the act of speaking is an act of inaction. Lopahin's repeated statements about the sale of the estate and the cherry orchard are offered in a 'plain language' that Madame Ranyevskaia and her family refuse to understand. Looking at the rules of conversational engagement and at how they are broken provides us with a methodical insight into the structure and ideological project of the text. This offers us a far more incisive approach than, for example, the essentially descriptive methodology pursued by Hayman (*et al.*), where comments on dialogue in *The Cherry Orchard* are limited to: 'the audience can gauge what is going on underneath the surface of irrelevant words' (1977: 32). This fails to account for how it is that the audience can register implied meanings and how irrelevance is dialogised. (See also Grice's 'co-operative principle' in the next section.)

When subjected to a language-based study, the dominant structural mark of dialogue in *The Cherry Orchard* is revealed as dichotomous and self-contradictory, i.e. as a combination of the nineteenth-century tradition of realistic dramatisations of society in conversation, and the twentieth-century pre-occupation with rule-breaking. Generically the play is also ambiguous (Chekhov originally intended the play as a comedy, Stanislavsky interpreted it as a tragedy), so it is hard to know how to read the refusal to sell the orchard: as comic, tragic, absurd? Given the mixed dialogic registers of rule observation and rule-breaking, it is perhaps reasonable to suppose that the play has more in common with the forthcoming age of anarchy than with the bourgeois century it left behind.

'RADICAL' DRAMA AND DIALOGUE

Where generically, comedy and tragedy have come closer together in the twentieth century, breaking down traditional structures in a mingling of tears and laughter, the underlying trend has been that of rule-breaking. In relation to dialogue, we should therefore expect to find a disruption of the traditional functions characteristic of dramatic speech, i.e. the means of establishing character, space and action, and to look for registers of disruption in the linguistic sign-system.

Modern play-texts characterised by rule-breaking modes which have, in formalist terms, 'made strange' the linguistic sign-system have attracted a good deal of critical attention. Burton's detailed study of naturally occurring conversations in modern drama (1980), for instance, draws readily on texts from Pinter and Ionesco, given that the work of these two playwrights consists to a conspicuous degree of 'small talk' which undermines the traditional expectation of external action moved forward through speech acts. Studies such as Burton's again help to show *how* the linguistic sign-system is transgressive (Burton's analysis draws on the linguistic analysis of everyday speech to show how it is used or abused in these 'deviant' texts), and offers a far more incisive and systematic way of seeing a text than, for example, the impressionistic readings of Pinter's work by John Russell Brown (1972: Chs 1, 2 & 3).

From our selection of plays, Beckett's *Endgame* provides a typical example of the linguistic sign-system 'made strange'. It was noted in Chapter 2 that dramatic exposition is conventionally concerned with the identification of characters. The opening sequence of *Endgame* observes none of these rules and conventions. Hamm and Clov do not engage in a dialogue which is structured to reveal adequate character histories or identities, or which accounts for the situation in which they find themselves as the play begins:

HAMM. Have you not had enough?

CLOV. Yes! (*Pause.*) Of what?

HAMM. Of this . . . this . . . thing.

CLOV. I always had. (*Pause.*) Not you?

HAMM. Then there's no reason for it to change.

(13)

It is unclear, and subsequently remains unclear, what 'this . . . thing' 'it' points to; there is no clarification of object reference. That the two speaker–listeners can engage in a series of illocutionary question–response acts which presuppose disambiguity where none exists is a parody of the normal rules of conversational engagement, and is ultimately 'meaningless' for the spectator-listener. This thwarts the maxim of 'meaningful' exchange in dramatic conversation where the spectator as listener expects to be fed information. For the spectator-listener, it is necessary to learn to 'read' and decode these transgressive acts, in order to 'make sense' of them. (This is not to be confused with interpreting or supplying 'meaning' as secondary critical 'readings' have frequently attempted to do in the case of Beckett's work.)

Because it is traditionally the function of dialogue to create the 'reality' of the dramatic universe and the protagonists within it as constant and consistent elements for the duration of the fiction, Beckett's use of dialogue may be read as a process of destabilisation. When, in *Hedda Gabler*, Miss Tesman refers to the sister and home that we do not 'see', we nevertheless accept that they 'exist' because they are 'said' to exist. The existence of Clov's offstage 'kitchen' is however negated by Hamm's statement that 'Outside of here it's death' (15).

If it is possible to decode the text as a multi-layered system of transgressive meanings, then the object of enquiry becomes the process whereby the lack of meaning or communication is established. Roger Fowler raises this point in the context of conversational analysis applied to *Waiting for Godot*, where the 'failures of communication' can be identified in the predominance of 'misfiring speech acts, misunderstandings, and incoherence' (1986: 116). In respect of this, it is useful to identify the abuse of the 'co-operative principle' identified by the language philosopher, Grice, as underlying meaningful conversational engagement. Grice identifies four preconditions:

1 *Quantity*, i.e. supply information as required but without excess.
2 *Quality*, i.e. to be truthful, not to lie or make an utterance without adequate data.
3 *Relation*, i.e. to be relevant.
4 *Manner*, i.e. to utter with precision and clarity, etc.

(1967: 47)

Where one or more of these rules is broken, then an unspoken or 'implied' meaning may be understood. 'Let's go to the public library', said by A to schoolfriend B in the presence of a parent when the friends have secretly arranged to meet in a cafe, flouts the second maxim. The 'implied' meaning, understood by friend B, is 'Let's go to the cafe.'

Beckett's text sets about thwarting the rules of conversational co-operation which enable statements to be made, to be understood, and to be responded to. Hamm is the main initiator of speech acts because, being blind and immobile, language is the only means through which he can 'act'. A large proportion

of these are *directives*, i.e. attempts to get someone to do something (Elam 1980: 167), delivered to Clov because he is the one
character capable of doing or acting. At one level, therefore, it
might be reasonable to suppose that Hamm is taking control,
that is, at initiating action through speech. At another, however, it becomes clear that the directives have no paralinguistic
context in which to make them purposeful. Nor does the dialogic exchange move the action on, because Hamm constantly
flouts the maxim of relevance, destroying conversational links:

HAMM. Why don't you kill me?

CLOV. I don't know the combination of the larder.

Pause.

HAMM. Go and get two bicycle-wheels.

(15)

On the other hand, Clov, who has both sight and movement, is
in a position to thwart the second maxim because Hamm cannot 'see' what is really going on. In the sequence with the toy
dog, for example, Hamm wants to know if the dog is standing,
and Clov answers that it is, when in fact the dog has fallen on
its side (30). Conversely, where the characters are able to make
sense of what is implied the spectator-listener is excluded.
Nagg's and Nell's reference to the crash on their tandem in
the Ardennes (19) implies knowledge of an unspoken, shared
past which is not shared with the spectator-listener.

In short, it is a dramatic discourse which relies entirely on a
mode of rule-breaking. In a dramatic world in which what is
said is unsaid ('In the morning they brace you up and in the
evening they calm you down. Unless it's the other way round.'
Hamm, 23), there is never any certainty as to 'meaning', openly
or implicitly stated, no way of knowing whether characters are
sincere or insincere. In this sense, the conventions of dialogue
in traditional tragedy and comedy, or the bourgeois patterns
of stage small-talk in nineteenth-century drama, are subverted,
undermined or overturned, to build a chaotic, dramatic universe through a linguistic sign-system signifying the absurd.

The nineteenth-century tradition of dialogue built on 'realistic' conversations is kept alive in the twentieth-century trend
of political drama in the wake of Osborne, Wesker, *et al.*
A more radical mode of political theatre, in terms of form

and content, takes its cue from the theory and practice of Brecht, where rules and conventions are broken in the process of communicating a political message.

The most startling and perhaps significant rule-breaking practice in terms of dialogue in this context is the use of the deictic marker 'I'. Catherine Belsey uses the concept of 'the split subject', derived from the psychoanalytic work of Jacques Lacan, in her analysis of the text which questions (the 'interrogative text'), to indicate how the division between 'the "I" who speaks and the "I" who is represented in the discourse' exploits this division or contradiction of the ego. This is in contrast to the 'classic realist text' where conflict is suppressed and the 'I' is fixed and stable (1980: 85). The point is well illustrated in the case of Vlasova's 'I' in *The Mother*. The opening dialogue constitutes an interrogation of the 'I' of the discourse, and it is precisely this process of self-examination which permits the 'I' who represents 'Pelagea Vlasova, a worker's widow and a worker's mother', to change and come to stand for the 'I' who represents 'The Mother'. Brecht's dialogue therefore demonstrates a radical departure from the 'I' who addresses a 'you' in the usual speaker–listener exchange. The 'I' who speaks addresses the 'I' of the discourse (reinforced in a performance context, where in a gestic or 'demonstrating' style of acting the 'I' of the performer is not submerged in the 'I' of the character).

The series of questions (directives) is followed through in the songs of the chorus, a plural voice which echoes the interrogative mode in sung verse form. Breaking into song is a further means of 'making strange' the mode of an I–You exchange; of shifting into an 'artistic' register which disrupts and interrupts the 'ordinary' spoken speech shared between two speakers, thereby drawing our attention to its content. (The use of songs may signify a change in pace, mood and so on as illustrated in *As You Like It*. For an example, see Act II, scene 5.) As in Greek tragedy, the use of a chorus marks a shift from the speech-interchange of individuals to a vocalisation of the community. In ideological terms, however, it should be noted that the two types of chorus exercise contrasting functions: whereas the Greek chorus confirms the values of the community, the Brechtian offers a means of challenging and changing them.

The use of a 'plural voice' is also found in Churchill's *Top Girls*, where the rule-breaking devices are used to politicise gender. Churchill's mode of cutting across or interrupting the I–You exchanges gives the appearance of 'natural' speech, where speakers do not necessarily wait until the end of a sentence before replying. Not surprisingly, this technique is revealed, on close examination, to be a highly structured and artificial process, where overlaps are 'timed' to increase pace, emotionality and so on. Whilst this structure of dialogue is widely used in Churchill's work, in *Top Girls* the use of overlap is a sign of the female voice. Brecht's splintering of the *ego* is further problematised in Churchill's text by the female entry into the symbolic order of language. As a logocentric or phallocentric sign-system (as identified in Derridean or Lacanian terms), language places the female subject in a marginalised relation to its patriarchal order. (For a detailed analysis, see Silverman 1983: Ch. 4, 'The Subject'.)

The stability of the I–You exchange which fixes identity in discourse is therefore fragmented in Churchill's restaurant scene where a babble of 'I's point not to the individual but to a collective female 'I', the object of patriarchal oppression. In the agency scenes, the female subject negotiates entry into language by assuming the position of a male subject. The dialogue between these empowered women is replete with signs of 'maleness', for example the use of sexual and scatological language. (On 'male language' see Lakoff 1975: 10.) The gender ambiguity of the subject is further signified in sentences such as Marlene's 'Could you please piss off', where the polite (female) request collides with the strong (male) directive, and the splintered fe/male subject enters no-wo/man's land. Alternatively, a rejection of (as opposed to a collusion with) language as a logo/phallocentric sign-system is signified by Pope Joan's vomiting of Latin, a spewing out of the words from which she is alienated by virtue of her 'true' sex.

Churchill's dialogue therefore foregrounds the destabilisation and displacement of the female subject in relation to language. In turn, this opens up a new area for dramatic research – gender and the linguistic sign-system in play scripts – and highlights the need to encode semiotic studies of dramatic dialogue and discourse from a feminist perspective.

5

STAGE DIRECTIONS I

Stage directions constitute a particularly underdeveloped topic, so it is our intention to offer a detailed treatment of these both in the present chapter and in Chapter 7. We shall begin here with an overview of extra- and intra-dialogic stage directions, and then proceed to classify and examine the functions of the various classes of direction. The chapter will conclude with a consideration of relevant historical and generic perspectives. Chapter 7 will consolidate this study of directions at the level of text by an examination of their implications for stage practice as a signifying system, parallel to the dialogue, which permits the reading out of setting and performance action, for example, from the text under rehearsal.

A cursory glance at the constituency of readers of the dramatic text will serve to explain why stage directions have in general been either ignored altogether or taken for granted and hence taken no further. They are customarily ignored by critics of a literary persuasion (see Eagleton 1986). Veltruský observes that such critics regard stage directions 'as something external to the play, something that does not really belong to its literary structure', a misperception which he takes to derive from the 'theory that a play is no more than the literary components of theatre' (1977: 41). Critics with a serious and informed interest in the *dramatic* operations of the play regularly interrogate the stage directions in the pursuit of a specific project, such as the laying bare of a sub-text (see, e.g., Gaskell 1972: 96–7), but this hardly constitutes a systematic analysis of the nature and functions of the directions. Theatrical practitioners, who have reason systematically to take full cognisance of the directions in a play-text under rehearsal, are rarely interested in committing the production process to writing. Moreover, where this does happen, the approach is likely to be discursive and anecdotal. Commendable exceptions (Brook 1968; Schechner 1988a) tend not to write at the level of close *textual* analysis.

For the casual and uninformed reader, as for critics whose orientation is narrowly literary, stage directions appear to do little more than impede the flow of the dramatic narrative. Hayman, asserting somewhat dogmatically that the concern of the directions is generally with action, suggests that 'the eye is liable to glide quickly and ungratefully' over the page (1977: 15). Reynolds, with regard to the extensive establishing stage directions that are characteristic of much nineteenth- and twentieth-century drama, notes that 'the temptation for the reader is often to pass over such detailed directions in the mistaken impression that the play begins with the opening lines of dialogue' (1986: 19). Given the status of the novel as the dominant literary form of the modern period, it is hardly surprising that the play-text is often read as a novel *manqué*. The casual reader has a conditioned investment in the pursuit of narrative pleasures which are guaranteed by a fictional 'contract'. The unproductive consequences of the play-as-novel approach – a deformed text, a disappointed reader – suggest, however, that habits of reading cannot be unproblematically transposed across differential forms. The dramatic text must be read on its own terms.

OVERVIEW

Dialogue/(extra-dialogic) stage directions

As noted in Chapter 4, Ingarden employs the terms *Haupttext* ('primary text') and *Nebentext* ('ancillary text') to differentiate between the dialogue of the characters and the stage directions which frame that dialogue (1973: 208). The choice of terms suggests parallel signifying systems, a parallelism which is formalised in the layout of the screenplay. In the dramatic text, however, the stage directions variously precede, are interspersed with or succeed the dialogue. Generally italicised and subject to a range of parenthetical conventions, they are set apart from the dialogue on the printed page.

Esslin notes that, of the printed play-text, only the *Haupttext* is 'available to the spectators of a performance as a producer of meaning' (1987: 80). The *Nebentext*, subject to interpretation by the director, designer, actors and technicians, adhered to with varying degrees of commitment and understanding, on occasion ignored, may or may not survive to inform the production.

For Esslin, drama is in essence 'mimetic *action*'. Hence he perceives a literary bias in the critical terminology adopted by Ingarden, and he is concerned to assert the primacy of the *Nebentext* over the *Haupttext* (ibid.: 83). Veltruský takes up the contrary position. He acknowledges that stage directions are integral to the 'literary structure' of the play and that they 'assume very important functions in its semantic construction'. But in relation to the dialogue, the position they occupy is a 'subordinate' one (1977: 47).

This question of precedence, ultimately unproductive, is symptomatic of the long-standing dispute between critics of a 'theatrical' or of a 'literary' orientation, in which either party seeks 'to make a virtue of its own *déformation professionelle*' (Bentley 1964: 148–9). A further impetus has been given to this dispute by the development of semiotic modes of analysis and the subsequent resistance to these on the part of theatrically oriented critics and theatrical practitioners. The proceedings of the 1983 Alsager seminar on 'Semiotics and the Theatre' illustrate the terms of this debate with some precision (see Hammond 1984). For the purposes of the present discussion it seems most useful to regard stage directions and dialogue, on the basis of Ingarden's parallel terms, as complementary and interdependent signifying systems. Stage directions frame the dialogue in two senses: literally, in the layout of the page, and theatrically, in that they impart to the printed text the status of a blueprint for theatrical production. The production team is offered a series of indications of the dramatist's theatrical intentions. The reader is offered the opportunity to read performance action from the text, and so to stage the play in a theatre of her/his imagination.

Stage directions (proper)/authorial narrative

Veltruský is concerned to make a distinction between stage directions proper and what he appears to regard as the dramatic equivalent of the authorial metatext (narrative voice/s) in the nineteenth-century realist novel.

He implies a *Haupttext–Nebentext* relationship by asserting that, at the level of the dramatic text, 'meanings are conveyed by two entirely different forms of language – the speeches attributed to the interlocutors and the author's notes (usually called stage directions)' (ibid.: 37). He goes on to point out that such 'notes' are 'sometimes called narrative', an appellation he endorses, albeit with the qualification that extensive notes tend toward a descriptive rather than a narrative function, as an index of length. He cites, as an extreme example, the scenarios of the Commedia dell'Arte, plot outlines which served as the basis of improvised performances and which therefore consist wholly of 'author's notes' (ibid.: 48–9).

While this distinction may be accepted, it is evident that in the modern period the dramatist frequently has recourse to extended passages of stage directions for the immediate issue of realising the text in performance. Act I of *Hedda Gabler* prefaces the dialogue with a prescriptive and carefully detailed description of the Tesmans' drawing-room, the setting for the play overall. In *Endgame* the lighting, setting and characters are sketched briefly, but the moves for Clov's establishing mime which follow are indicated in precise detail. Moreover, a dramatic text may be constituted solely by stage directions. Beckett's *Acts Without Words* I and II, and *Quad*, short mimes written respectively for theatre and television, again provide detailed and precise moves for the performer, who is required to do no more (nor less) than follow them precisely.

Veltruský observes that texts such as the Commedia scenarios 'are perceived by the reader not as works of literature but as mere librettos, mere materials that can be used to construct a work of art. They are made up only of the secondary components of a literary genre and do not comprise the dominant component capable of carrying the esthetic function' (ibid.: 49). The repeated use of 'mere' and the relegation of the *Nebentext* to a position of subordination reveal clearly the literary orientation of the writer. Segre, in contrast, treats the stage directions which constitute the texts of *Acts Without Words* as literary devices in their own right, exercising a poetic function which warrants examination (Elam 1980: 217–18). In the plays of

Beckett and Stoppard, moreover, the stage directions frequently operate in playful modes which complement the operations of the dialogue, and might therefore be read as a celebration of the possibilities of slippage between *Nebentext* and *Haupttext*. The example is taken from *Endgame*:

HAMM. Order!

CLOV (*straightening up*). I love order. It's my dream. A world where all would be silent and still and each thing in its last place, under the last dust.

He starts picking up again.

(39)

The interest of such projects lies in the implication that the dual identity of the dramatic text, its simultaneous existence as literary artifact and as blueprint for production, may be argued with regard to the stage directions – the guarantors, as it were, of the text's theatrical potential – themselves. To view the directions as in some sense literary devices is not, of course, to detract from their primary theatrical function.

Extra-/intra-dialogic stage directions

A third distinction remains to be made. A cursory glance at the text of a classical or medieval or renaissance play reveals the significant absence of a register of stage directions operating in parallel to the dialogue. The general critical position on texts of the earlier periods is that stage directions are (1) minimal, and (2) non-prescriptive. We shall deal with the historical perspective in the final section of this chapter. For present purposes it is sufficient to cite Esslin's view, not atypical, that the *Nebentext* is 'very often altogether absent (as, for example, in the texts of Greek plays that have come down to us) or extremely scanty and vague (as in the stage directions of Elizabethan drama)' (1987: 80). This leads him dogmatically to assert that a modern director or production team is compelled to 'create' a *Nebentext* of their own. Clearly such a course is open to the director or production team. Stanislavsky, for example, added his own aural and pictorial sub-text to the plays of Chekhov, texts already extensively supplied with the dramatist's own stage directions (see Braun 1982: Ch. 5).

With regard to the earlier periods, we would dissent from the view that the director must labour under the obligation of *ex nihilo* creation, and we would argue that from the perspective of a basic understanding of the conventions of performance and production obtaining at a given moment in the history of the theatre the reading of performance action *from the text* is a logical and straightforward proceeding. The text itself, on this view, states the terms of its own staging. It follows that a second register of stage directions may be perceived *within*, and be extrapolated from, the dialogue itself. We shall use the term 'intra-dialogic' to denote this register of directions, 'extra-dialogic' to denote the directions which are set apart from the dialogue on the page.

A brief analysis of the opening exchanges of *Oedipus the King*, between Oedipus and the Priest, will serve to illustrate our argument. It should be noted that the few italicised stage directions printed alongside the Fagles version are the translator's own extrapolations and conjectures from the dialogue. (Line and not page references are cited in the extract and the analysis which follows.)

OEDIPUS.

Oh my children, the new blood of ancient Thebes,
why are you here? Huddling at my altar,
praying before me, your branches wound in wool.
Our city reeks with the smoke of burning incense,
rings with cries for the Healer and wailing for the dead. 5
I thought it wrong, my children, to hear the truth
from others, messengers. Here I am myself –
you all know me, the world knows my fame:
I am Oedipus.
                    Speak up, old man, Your years,
your dignity – you should speak for the others.   10
Why here and kneeling, what preys upon you so?
Some sudden fear? some strong desire?
You can trust me. I am ready to help,
I'll do any thing. I would be blind to misery
not to pity my people kneeling at my feet.   15

PRIEST.

Oh Oedipus, king of the land, our greatest power!
You see us before you now, men of all ages

clinging to your altars. Here are boys,
still too weak to fly from the nest,
and here the old, bowed down with the years,   20
the holy ones – a priest of Zeus myself – and here
the picked, unmarried men, the young hope of Thebes.
And all the rest, your great family gathers now,
branches wreathed, massing in the squares,
kneeling before the two temples of queen Athena   25
or the river-shrine where the embers glow and die
and Apollo sees the future in the ashes.
                                                    Our city –
look around you, see with your own eyes –
our ship pitches wildly, cannot lift her head
from the depths, the red waves of death . . .   30
Thebes is dying. A blight on the fresh crops
and the rich pastures, cattle sicken and die,
and the women die in labor, children stillborn,
and the plague, the fiery god of fever hurls down
on the city, his lightning slashing through us –   35
raging plague in all its vengeance, devastating
the house of Cadmus! And black Death luxuriates
in the raw, wailing miseries of Thebes.

The action of the play is located in the central Greek state of
Thebes, before the royal house, the palace of Oedipus and
Jocasta. This is represented by the stage-building (*skene*), a
two-storey edifice with central double doors giving on to a
low, raised stage. The front wall offered a neutral architectural
façade and could therefore assume such fictional location(s)
as a particular play might require. A flight of steps led down
from the stage to a dancing-circle (*orchestra*) some sixty feet in
diameter, at ground level. An altar of Dionysus, the patron deity
of Athenian drama, stood at its centre. A vast tiered auditorium,
perhaps seating 14,000 spectators, rose up from the periphery of
the orchestra at the front and to the sides of the stage.

    Oedipus the King begins in spectacular fashion. A large group
of supernumeraries enter from stage left, along the gangway
formed by the retaining wall of the auditorium and the adjacent
front corner of the stage. Conventionally, such an entrance
denoted that they had come from the nearby city; an entrance
from stage right denoted a journey from farther afield, such as

Creon's return from his mission to Delphi (91–6). The group entry is sombre in mood. The supernumeraries play the collective role of a delegation of suppliants, seeking to enlist the assistance of Oedipus in relieving Thebes from the plague with which the city is afflicted. Their suppliant status is apparent from the 'branches wound in wool' which they carry (3). They represent a cross-section of the city's male population: 'men of all ages' (17), 'boys still too weak to fly the nest' (18–19), 'the old, bowed down with the years' (20), 'priests' (21), and 'unmarried men, the young hope of Thebes' (22). They form a tableau vivant, 'huddling' at altars (2), 'clinging' to them (18), 'kneeling' before the palace (11, 15) in attitudes of prayer (3), and await the arrival of Oedipus. The number of altars used is uncertain. Religious propriety may have precluded the use of the altar of Dionysus. At a later stage of the play, Jocasta makes her pragmatic offering to Apollo on an on-stage altar (1007–9), and it is likely that this is one of several. It is possible, also, that incense-burners were placed in view of the spectators (94), and that the suppliants both called upon Apollo (5), under his epithet of 'Healer of Delos' (173), and uttered lamentations for the dead (5).

When the scene is established, pictorially and atmospherically, Oedipus enters formally from the palace. His rank is denoted by costume, his gender by the colour of the mask. By convention, male characters wore terracotta masks, female characters white. Rank was also indexed by the degree of elaboration of the hair-dress. Oedipus is presumably attended by guards (162–3), a further index of status, and may walk with a limp (1031–6). In the first speech of the conventionally expositional prologue, Oedipus identifies the suppliants (1–3), the setting (1), the atmosphere (4–5) and himself (7–9). He creates an initial impression of responsible government (6–7, 11–15), and singles out the priest of Zeus (21) as spokesperson for the delegation (9–10). The priest responds to Oedipus on behalf of the city at large, shifting the focus of attention from the stage picture to an imaginary world of suffering. He describes city-wide acts of supplication (23–7), and delineates in insistently imagistic terms the impact of pestilence and plague (27–38).

We shall return to issues around the reading of performance action from the text in Chapter 7.

CLASSIFICATION

The present section provides a classification of the various types of stage direction, and an examination of their characteristic functions. There also remain for consideration a number of conventions which relate to, and reinforce the functions of, the stage directions. We shall deal with these first.

The published version of *Top Girls*, a 'fully revised, post-production edition', supplements the play-text with the following materials:

1 Caryl Churchill's acknowledgement of her use of two source-books.
2 Details of the date, venue and cast of the first production.
3 The locations of the play's five scenes, and the times of the action.
4 Prefatory notes on the five characters drawn from history, painting and literature.
5 Notes on the conventions used to denote modes of overlapping speech.

The acknowledgement of a dramatist's sources is unusual, and to be welcomed, in that it facilitates both the further investigation of the play's content and the exploration of the process and strategies of adaptation. The next two items derive from the programme for the first production and serve, respectively, to indicate that all roles with the single exception of that of Marlene may be doubled or trebled, and that the play's five scenes take place in four locations and move conventionally forward in time until the final scene, which takes place 'a year earlier'. The final sets of notes serve to clarify quite radical compositional devices. The guests at Marlene's dinner-party, which constitutes the play's opening scene, are drawn variously from ninth-, thirteenth- and nineteenth-century history (Pope Joan, Lady Nijo, Isabella Bird), a Brueghel painting (Dull Gret) and a Chaucerian tale (Patient Griselda). The interplay of this group of characters operates both to foreground the transhistorical and transcultural aspects of women's oppression and to deconstruct the terms of gender representation in dominant cultural production. The overlapping dialogue is intended to replicate the relative disorder of actual speech interaction in circumstances of festivity or agitation.

Details of the first production, and explanatory notes by the dramatist, are increasingly regular concomitants of the published version of a new play. Such information, in conjunction with the stage directions, is likely to position the reader in a more secure relationship with the text. The same observation may be made of the formal ordering of the characters (*dramatis personae*) which customarily precedes the opening scene. The information given for the characters in *The Cherry Orchard* deals with names, including patronymics and 'pet' names, positions, ages and familial relationships. For example:

RANYEVSKAIA, Liubov Andryeevna (Liuba), a landowner

ANIA (Anichka), her daughter, aged 17

VARIA (Varvara Mihailovna), her adopted daughter, aged 24

GAYEV, Leonid Andryeevich (Lionia), brother of Mme Ranyevskaia.

The use of the French title reminds us that French was the preferred language of the Russian aristocracy at the time of writing (1903).

Veltruský reads the names of the characters as authorial 'annotations', suggesting that, where there is a causal link between name and character, the appearance in the printed text of the character's name before all of her/his speeches 'automatically adheres its meaning' and so conditions the response of the reader (1977: 41, 45). The personified abstractions of the medieval morality play and the humoresque characters of Jacobean drama constitute cases in point. Included among the dramatis personae of *Everyman* are Death, Good Deeds, Confession and Five Wits. Jonson's *Bartholomew Fair* offers among others John Littlewit, Dame Purecraft, Zeal-of-the-Land Busy and Humphrey Wasp.

Brechtian theatre makes insistent use of captions and song-titles, in the manner of the inter-titles of silent cinema. In *The Mother*, captions are variously employed to anticipate the action of a scene, or to indicate its mode of operation, location or historical context:

4 PELAGEA VLASOVA IS GIVEN HER FIRST LESSON IN ECONOMICS (20)
5 REPORT ON THE 1ST MAY, 1905 (23)

6 THE TEACHER VESOVCHIKOV'S FLAT IN ROSTOV (26)
8 IN THE SUMMER OF 1905 THE COUNTRY WAS SHAKEN BY PEASANT
  UPRISINGS AND AGRICULTURAL STRIKES (39)

Songs and verses for recitation are often given titles, and these are comparably straightforward: for example SONG OF THE ANSWER; IN PRAISE OF THE REVOLUTIONARY (9–10; 33). Both captions and titles of songs and verses may be incorporated into production, either announced by the actors or signalled by means of placard, projection or news-panel, as further distanciation devices.

Mention might be made also of the author's note at the beginning of *Everyman* which offers, in addition to an encapsulation of the play's narrative content, a generic marker:

> HERE BEGINNETH A TREATISE HOW THE HIGH FATHER OF HEAVEN
> SENDETH DEATH TO SUMMON EVERY CREATURE TO COME AND
> GIVE ACCOUNT OF THEIR LIVES IN THIS WORLD, AND IS IN MANNER
> OF A MORAL PLAY.
>
> (207)

The tabular classification of intra- and extra-dialogic stage directions which follows will address sequentially the identification and physical and vocal definition of character, conventions of delivery, design elements and technical elements. Chapter 7 will take up these issues in relation to the theatrical context of the directions, examining their significance for the work of the actor, the designer and lighting designer, and the technician, and for that of the director in her/his orchestration of the production overall.

The following abbreviations apply:

OK	: *Oedipus the King*	HG:	*Hedda Gabler*
Ev	: *Everyman*	CO:	*The Cherry Orchard*
AY	: *As You Like It*	M :	*The Mother*
P	: *Phaedra*	En :	*Endgame*
LA	: *Lady Audley's Secret*	TG :	*Top Girls*

Table 5.1 Classification of stage directions

	1. *Character: identification*	
Function	Intra-dialogic	Extra-dialogic
1. Identification/ description at first entrance	*Ev* 209 DEATH: 'Everyman, stand still! Whither art thou going/Thus gaily?'	*LA* 239 '*Enter* SIR MICHAEL AUDLEY, *a grey-headed gentleman of 70, arm in arm with* LADY AUDLEY, *supposed to be about 24.*'
2. Detailed description at or prior to first entrance	*P* 154 OENONE: 'The queen is almost at her destined end./. . . She's dying from a hidden malady;/Eternal discord reigns within her mind./Her restless anguish tears her from her bed.'	*HG* 289 '. . . BRACK . . . *is a man of forty-five, square but well built and light in his movements. His face is roundish, with a fine profile. His hair, still almost black, is short and carefully waved. His eyes are lively and bright. His eyebrows are thick and so is his moustache with its clipped ends. He is dressed in a well-cut outdoor suit – a little too young for his age. He wears an eye-glass, which he now and then lets fall.*'
3. Occupation	*OK* 174 LEADER: 'Lord Tiresias sees with the eyes of Lord Apollo./Anyone searching for truth, my king,/might learn it from the prophet, clear as day.'	*M* 40 '*Two strike-breakers sit eating and talk to the estate butcher.*'
4. Dominant trait(s)	*TG* 86 JOYCE: 'What about Angie? . . . She's stupid, lazy and frightened . . .'	*CO* 340 'GAYEV, *as he comes in, moves his arms and body as if he were playing billiards.*'

Table 5.1 Continued

1. Character: identification		
Function	*Intra-dialogic*	*Extra-dialogic*
5. Relationship to other(s)	*En* 15 HAMM: 'Accursed progenitor!' (*To* NAGG)	*CO* 347 'FEERS (*Brushing* GAYEV, *admonishing him).*'

2. Character: physical definition		
6. Entrance	*OK* 162–3 PRIEST: 'Creon's just arriving . . . he's crowned, look,/and the laurel wreath is bright with berries.'	*LA* 251 '*Enter* LUKE MARKS, R.C., *flushed with drink.*'
7. Exit	*P* 189 THESEUS: 'Let us go in and end this grim suspense./Let us discover criminal and crime,/And Phaedra tell us why she is distraught.'	*HG* 290 '*Mutual good-byes.* MRS ELVSTED *and* HEDDA *go out by the hall door.*'
8. Manner	*P* 38 ROSALIND: 'Look you, who comes here,/A young man and an old in solemn talk.'	*LA* 245 'LADY AUDLEY (*throwing off her levity of manner, and reflecting).*'
9. Carriage	*CO* 349 PISHCHIK: 'So you're going to bed now? Och, my gout! I'd better stay the night here.'	*En* 11 'CLOV *goes and stands under window left, Stiff, staggering walk.*'
10. Posture	*M* 56 THE DOCTOR: 'She's completely exhausted and on no account should she get up. She's an old woman after all.'	*CO* 385 'LIUBOV ANDRYEEVNA . . . *sits hunched up in a chair, crying bitterly.*'
11. Gesture	*Ev* 232 EVERYMAN: 'Into thy hands, Lord, my soul I commend.'	*HG* 301 'HEDDA (*with a gesture of disagreement).*'

Table 5.1 Continued

2. *Character: physical definition*		
Function	*Intra-dialogic*	*Extra-dialogic*
12. Movement	*OK* 177 OEDIPUS: 'For the love of god, don't turn away,/ not if you know something. We beg you,/. . . on our knees.'	*En* 51 'CLOV *halts, without turning.*'
13. Action: self-directed	*En* 45 HAMM: 'Perhaps I could throw myself out on the floor.'	*TG* 35 'KIT *puts her hand under her dress, brings it out with blood on her finger.*'
14. Action: other-directed	*HG* 296 BRACK: 'No, no, no! Don't stand there aiming straight at me.'	*CO* 373 'ANIA . . . *runs to her mother, gives her a hug . . .*'
15. Action: self & object	*AY* 61 ORLANDO: 'Hang there my verse, in witness of my love . . .'	*M* 19 'SMILGIN *tries to hide his leaflet in his pocket.*'
16. Action: other & object	*HG* 345 HEDDA: 'Now I am burning your child, Thea. . . . Your child and Ejlert Lövberg's.'	*En* 16 'CLOY *pushes* NAGG *back into the bin. Closes the lid.*'
17. Reaction	*P* 206 THESEUS: 'Your colour changes and you seem aghast.'	*TG* 19 '*They are quite drunk. They get the giggles.*'
18. Dumb show	*OK* 159 OEDIPUS: 'Oh my children, new blood of ancient Thebes,/why are you here? Huddling at my altar,/praying before me, your branches wound in wool.'	*LA* 239 '*Enter* VILLAGERS, *followed by* MORRIS DANCERS, *C., who perform a dance and exeunt.*'

84

Table 5.1 Continued

| | 3. *Character: vocal definition* | |
Function	Intra-dialogic	Extra-dialogic
19. Facial expression	*P* 156 PHAEDRA: 'Oenone, blushes sweep across my face;/My grievous shame stands all too clear revealed,/And tears despite me fill my aching eyes.'	*CO* 386 'LIUBOV ANDRYEEVNA *is not crying but her face is pale and tremulous.*'
20. Mode of delivery	*OK* 211 JOCASTA: '. . . I turn to you, Apollo, you are nearest,/I come with prayers and offerings . . . I beg you,/cleanse us, set us free of defilement.'	*M* 44 'IN PRAISE OF VLASOVA, *recited by the estate builder and his people.*'
21. Tone: quality of voice	*AY* 76 ORLANDO: 'Your accent is something finer than you could purchase in so removed a dwelling.'	*CO* 396 'YEPIHODOV (*in a husky voice*).'
22. Tone: emotion	*OK* 223 JOCASTA: 'Aieeeeee/– man of agony –/this is the only name I have for you,/that, no other – ever, ever, ever!'	*CO* 336 'LIUBOV ANDRYEEVNA (*joyfully, through her tears*).'
23. Pace	*Ev* 230 BEAUTY: 'I cross out all this; adieu, by Saint John!/I take my cap in my lap, and am gone.'	*M* 15 'VLASOVA . . . *goes up to the entrance and speaks quickly.*'
24. Volume	*LA* 264 PHOEBE: 'I will proclaim you as a murderess! Help! help! Murder! Help! help!'	*M* 11 'PAVEL, *loudly to distract the commissioner:*'

Table 5.1 Continued

3. Character: vocal definition		
Function	*Intra-dialogic*	*Extra-dialogic*
25. Rhythm	CO 392 PISCHIK: 'Och, let me get my breath . . . 'I'm worn out. . . . My good friends . . . Give me some water . . .'	En 52 'HAMM . . . *(He repeats, chanting.)*'
26. Mannerism	TG 29 ISABELLA: 'So off I went to visit the Berber sheikhs in full blue trousers and great brass spurs.'	CO 339 'YASHA *(crossing the stage, in an affectedly genteel voice).*'
27. Emphasis	En 22 NAGG: 'But my dear Sir . . . look . . . at the world . . . and look . . . at my TROUSERS!'	HG 265 'MISS TESMAN. Oh it's not *that* kind of doctor he is. *(With a nod full of meaning.)*'
28. Non-verbal	LA 248 LADY AUDLEY: 'Dead men tell no tales! I am free! I am free! I am free! Ha, ha, ha!'	HG 292 'HEDDA *(to* BRACK, *laughing with a touch of contempt).*'
29. Role-within-role	CO 372 CHARLOTTA: . . . 'How charming you are, quite delightful. VOICE: And I like you very much also, Madam.'	En 21 'NAGG: Let me tell it again. *(Raconteur's voice)* . . . *(Tailor's voice)* . . . *(Customer's voice)* . . .'
4. Speech: formal concerns		
30. Addressee: self	TG 35 NELL: 'You're talking to yourself, sunshine.'	CO 398 '*(The stage is empty . . .* FEERS *appears . . .)* . . . *(Mutters something unintelligible.)*'
31. Addressee: other	Ev 223 CONFESSION: 'I know your sorrow well, Everyman.'	HG 319 'LÖVBORG *(to* HEDDA, *after a little pause).*'

Table 5.1 Continued

4. Speech: formal concerns		
Function	*Intra-dialogic*	*Extra-dialogic*
32. Addressee: audience	*AY* 131 ROSALIND: 'It is not the fashion to see the lady in the epilogue . . .'	*LA* 23 'REPORT ON THE 1ST MAY, 1905'
33. Aside	*En* 49 HAMM: 'An aside, ape! Did you never hear an aside before?'	*LA* 253 'LADY AUDLEY *(aside)*. What does he mean? *(Aloud.)* Heart's-ease?'
34. Silence/pause	*OK* 171 OEDIPUS: 'Next,/if anyone knows the murderer is a stranger,/a man from alien soil, come, speak up.'	*En* 46 'CLOV: Is your throat sore? *(Pause.)* Would like a lozenge? *(Pause.)* No? *(Pause.)* Pity.'
35. Song	*LA* 238 LUKE: '. . . marry thee and drive thee to market in my shay cart, singing/"Gee wo, Dobbin, . . ./Gee up and gee wo".'	*M* 50 'CHORUS, *sung by the Revolutionary Workers to Vlasova:*'

5. Design elements		
36. Setting: place	*AY* 38 ROSALIND: 'Well this is the Forest of Arden.'	*TG* 33 'JOYCE'S *back yard.*'
37. Setting: stage picture	*CO* 347 LIUBOV ANDRYEEVNA: 'I used to sleep in this nursery; I used to look on the orchard from here. . . . All, all white!'	*TG* 33 '*The house with back door is upstage. Downstage a shelter made of junk, made by children.*'
38. Stage levels/areas	*Ev* 207 GOD: 'I perceive, here in my majesty,/How that all creatures be to me unkind.'	*CO* 370 '*Adjoining the drawing-room at the back, and connected to it by an archway, is the ballroom.*'

Table 5.1 Continued

	5. Design elements	
Function	Intra-dialogic	Extra-dialogic
39. Onstage/offstage relationship	OK 160 PRIEST: 'And all the rest, your great family gathers now,/. . . massing in the squares,/ kneeling before the two temples of queen Athena/or the river shrine . . .'	HG 296 'HEDDA (looking down the garden and calling) . . . BRACK (is heard from below, at a little distance).'
40. Offstage geography	En 12 CLOV: 'I'll go now to my kitchen, ten feet by ten feet by ten feet, and wait for him to visit me.'	LA 260 'A . . . flight of steps, supposed to lead to a hayloft.'
41. Time: of day	M 9 VLASOVA: 'Pavel, it'd be very awkward for me if the landlord noticed people getting together here at five o'clock in the morning and printing things.'	CO 334 'It is early morning: the sun is just coming up.'
42. Time: season	CO 395 LOPAHIN: 'Do you remember, last year about this time it was snowing already, but now it's quite still and sunny.'	HG 263 '. . . a veranda outside and autumn foliage.'
43. Time: relative to play overall	AY 100 ORLANDO: 'I must attend the Duke at dinner. By two o'clock I will be with you again.'	TG 66 'Scene two. A year earlier.'

Table 5.1 Continued

| | 5. *Design elements* | |
Function	*Intra-dialogic*	*Extra-dialogic*
44. Costume: distinctive marks	*AY* 48 JAQUES: 'I met a fool i' the forest,/ A motley fool.'	*En* 12 *'In a dressing-gown, a stiff toque on his head, a large blood-stained handkerchief over his face, a whistle hanging, from his neck, a rug over his knees . . .* HAMM.'
45. Costume: occasion-specific	*Ev* 225 KNOWLEDGE: 'It is a garment of sorrow:/. . ./ Contrition it is.'	*HG* 296 'BRACK, *dressed as for an informal party. . . . He is carrying a light overcoat on his arm.'*
46. Costume: disguise/role-within-role	*AY* 28 CELIA: 'I'll put myself in poor and mean attire./And with a kind of umber smirch my face.'	*AY* 37 *'Enter* ROSALIND *as* GANYMEDE, CELIA *as* ALIENA *and* TOUCHSTONE.'
47. Properties: movable	*OK* 160 PRIEST: 'You see us before you now, . . ./clinging to your altars.'	*M* 30 *'*VESOVCHIKOV, *in front of a blackboard:'*
48. Properties: personal	*En* 30 CLOV: 'But he isn't finished, I tell you! First you finish your dog and then you put on his ribbon!'	*CO* 337 *'Enter* VARIA *with a bunch of keys at her waist.'*

	6. *Technical elements*	
49. Lighting: offstage source	*HG* 273 HEDDA: 'Oh! The maid has gone and opened the veranda door! there's a perfect flood of sunshine coming in.'	*HG* 263 *'The sun shines in through the glass doors.'*
50. Lighting: onstage source	*M* 45 VESOVCHIKOV: 'The lamp's falling off the wall in my room.'	*LA* 261 'LUKE . . . *(. . . trying to light his pipe from candle on table.)'*

Table 5.1 Continued

| | 6. Technical elements | |
Function	Intra-dialogic	Extra-dialogic
51. Lighting: mood	*HG* 273 HEDDA: 'Just draw the blinds, my dear, will you? That gives a softer light.'	*En* 11 'Bare interior. Grey light.'
52. Lighting: effects	*LA* 262 LUKE: 'Oh mercy – mercy! help! help! The fire grows stronger and stronger.'	*LA* 260 'Window in flat, showing moonlight perspective.'
53. Lighting: time of day	*P* 155 PHAEDRA: 'My eyes are dazzled by the daylight's glare.'	*HG* 263 'Morning light.'
54. Lighting: season	*CO* 334 YEPIHODOV: 'There's a frost outside, three degrees of it, and the cherry trees are covered in bloom.'	*HG* 263 '. . . a glass door . . . . Through its panes can be seen . . . autumn foliage.'
55. Sound: onstage, character-related	*M* VESOVCHIKOV: 'I'm afraid your printing illegal publications here is quite impossible if it's going to make such a noise.'	*CO* 344 'VARIA . . . (Picks out a key and unlocks an old bookcase with a jingling noise.)'
56. Sound: offstage, character-related	*CO* 335 LOPAHIN: 'Yes, they really are coming! Let's go and meet them at the door.'	*HG* 363 'HEDDA goes into the inner room and draws the curtains after her. . . . Suddenly she is heard playing a wild dance tune on the piano.'
57. Sound: offstage, external	*CO* 365 LIUBOV ANDRYEEVNA: 'What was that? LOPAHIN: I don't know. Somewhere a long way off a lift cable in one of the mines must have broken.'	*M* 17 'The factory siren. The workers stand up to go back to work.'

HISTORIC AND GENERIC PERSPECTIVES

In terms of the aesthetics of performance, the history of theatrical production may be divided broadly into three phases, respectively characterised by the operations of conventionalism, by the cultivation of illusion and by the contestation of illusionism.

1. The first phase, which spans a period of some 2,000 years, from the civic institutionalisation of drama in Athens in the late sixth century BC to the development of the European open-air theatres of the fifteenth and sixteenth centuries, is marked by outdoor performance, community attendance and a religious dimension, by poetic and often densely layered texts, by the overt self-presentation of the actor *as* actor and by a set of functionalistic performance conventions: for example, masks decorated to denote gender and status on the Greek stage, adjacent 'mansions' representing Heaven and Hell in medieval scenic disposition, and the use of torches and the music of 'hautbois' respectively to signpost nocturnal and interior scenes in the Elizabethan public playhouse. On such stages, the spectator perceives a real actor, and is impelled by the interdependent operation of textual and performance conventions to imagine an *imaginary* Oedipus, Everyman or Rosalind. The actor, as the opening chorus of *Henry V* insistently notes, serves as a 'cipher' or symbol in what is in effect a moral and/or religious demonstration, and so 'works' on the 'imaginary forces' of the spectator. In turn, the spectator is invited to work, in a creative collusion with dramatist and actor, towards a more complete realisation of the enacted text.

2. The second phase, which is initiated by the private theatres of the late Renaissance and which constitutes the dominant theatrical mode of the modern period, is marked by indoor performance, an entrepreneurial basis – and in consequence class-delimited audiences – and a secular orientation, and by the naturalistic project which sought to represent life on stage with a photographic exactitude. To this end is developed the 'fourth wall' convention, which in conjunction with the deployment of artificial lighting (candles, gas, electricity) demarcates a fixed boundary between performance space and audience space, and successive regimens of actor-training designed to

blur distinctions between the actor and the role. The spectator position thus constructed is both voyeuristic and identificatory. Drawn into the coherent fictional world of the narrative and into acts of identification with the dramatis personae, the spectator is now complicitly passive, her/his pleasure predicated upon a 'willing suspension of disbelief' (Coleridge 1907, II:6). It goes almost without saying that the texts of illusionistic theatre, the project of which is the analogous reproduction of everyday speech, are non-poetic, the development of a symbolic sub-text by the naturalistic dramatists Ibsen and Chekhov and an expressionistic poetry *of* the theatre by playwrights such as Strindberg and Pirandello notwithstanding.

3. The third phase is marked by an anti-illusionistic aesthetic posited upon the foregrounding of the means of representation in order to maintain a critical distance between spectator and performance. Associated particularly with the stage practice of Meyerhold and his co-workers in post-revolutionary Russia and that of Piscator and Brecht in Germany during the 1920s and the early 1930s (see Braun 1982: Chs 8–11), explicitly didactic and mobilised in the service of specific social and political imperatives, this aesthetic of distanciation reflects to a very considerable extent a return to the convention-based modes of presentation of the Greek, medieval and Elizabethan theatres. Brecht, arguably the most influential of modern stage practitioners, was a theorist and a prolific dramatist also. With regard both to stagecraft and to dramatic composition, he acknowledged direct debts to the Elizabethan theatre (Brecht 1965: 57–64; see also Heinemann 1985), itself a primary site for the transmission of classical forms. Moreover, in the *Lehrstücke* and in the 'parables' for the theatre there may be discerned a conception of the social function of the dramatist and an emphasis on the conjunction of pleasure and instruction which call to mind the self-conscious reflections of the Aristophanic chorus (Aristophanes 1964: 149; see also Dover 1972: Ch. 4). Within this anti-illusionistic tradition which – perhaps unjustly, given earlier, seminal work in Russia – has come to receive the generic designation 'Brechtian', the spectator is again accorded an active role. Performance is offered frankly *as* performance, and the lure of emotional identification, on the part of both actor and spectator, with fictional constructs is in consequence countered. The attention of the spectator, rather, is

now directed outwards, from the enactment to the social reality inscribed therein.

A direct correlation is to be established, therefore, between the aesthetics of performance, as posited in this three-phase model of the history of theatrical production, and the textual taxonomy demonstrated in the preceding chapter:

Theatre aesthetic	*Textual form*
1 Operations of conventionalism	Classic: *OK, Ev, AY, P*
2 Cultivation of illusion	Bourgeois: *LA, HG, CO*
3 Contestation of illusionism	Radical: *M, En, TG*

It follows that there is an association to be made between specific theatrical and dramatic forms and specific modes and types of stage direction.

Reference has already been made to a certain critical myopia with regard to the operation of the intra-dialogic mode of stage direction in the 'classic' text. A severe form of the condition is apparent in the following formulation: 'Some of the very best playwrights, like Shakespeare, give very little information in stage directions' (Hayman 1977: 68). Esslin, as has been noted, is of the opinion that the modern director is obliged of necessity to furnish a *Nebentext* of her/his own devising. While our departure from such views need not be urged further, it is clearly evident both from the analysis of the opening exchanges of *Oedipus the King* and from the parallel tabulation of intra- and extra-dialogic modes of direction, that the former work, in the 'classic' text, to perform a series of functions *equivalent* to those performed by the latter in the 'bourgeois' text.

The shift from phase one to phase two is marked by the emergence of the extra-dialogic mode of stage direction, as a function of the development of illusionistic theatre; the shift from phase two to phase three by the subversion of that mode to place emphasis on theatre *as* theatre and so to break the illusionistic frame. In the first case, detailed directions for physical and vocal characterisation, for example, work to further the project of analogical representation which defines the 'bourgeois' text. A congruent observation may be made with regard to the development of scenic and technical resources. It is readily apparent from the tabular classification that the examples of extra-dialogic direction selected to illustrate design, and lighting and sound effects, are drawn preponderantly from the three 'bourgeois' texts: *Lady Audley's Secret*; *Hedda Gabler* and *The Cherry Orchard*. In the second case, the directions are to a marked degree self-referential. Over and above a customary concern with the aesthetic dimension of the envisaged production, the issue of *pitch*, the manner in which the production is addressed to the spectator, is now foregrounded. It is to the self-conscious theatricality of the 'radical' text that the reader's attention is thereby drawn.

We are now in a position to summarise the discussion in relation to the *Haupttext-Nebentext* distinction formulated by Ingarden.

1. The 'classic' text operates at the level of the *Haupttext*. It consists almost wholly of dialogue. The dialogue simultaneously performs the work of stage directions and, as has been demonstrated with regard to the opening exchange of *Oedipus the King*, the extrapolation of an intra-dialogic *Nebentext* is a logical and straightforward undertaking.

2. The 'bourgeois' text operates at the levels both of *Haupttext* and explicit *Nebentext*. It is apparent from the tabular classification that much information continues to be offered in the intra-dialogic mode, both to counterpoint and to supplement the extra-dialogic directions.

3. The 'radical' text operates at both levels also. Here, in contradistinction to the 'bourgeois' text, the directions work to inscribe a form of theatricality which calls attention to its status *as* theatricality. The consequence for theatrical realisation is that the stage–spectator relationship constructed by illusionistic theatre, the dominant form of the modern period, is deconstructed and, hence, subverted.

4. Two extreme positions may be noted briefly. Firstly, as a function of the conditions of performance which obtained for French (neo-)classical tragedy, a text such as *Phaedra* operates virtually at the level of *Haupttext* only. Minimal information on character representation or performance action is offered intra-dialogically. Secondly, texts such as the Commedia dell'Arte scenarios or the Beckett mimes consist wholly of author's notes or extra-dialogic directions, and therefore operate at the level of *Nebentext* only.

Some general observations remain to be made with regard to the generic implications of extra-dialogic stage directions in plays of the modern period. In the case of the 'bourgeois' text, a broad distinction may be drawn between visual and verbal emphases. In *The Cherry Orchard*, for example, the clumsiness of the lovelorn Yepihodov and the idiosyncratic behaviour of the displaced Charlotta are exploited for comic effect. The directions, on occasion supported by dialogue, are thus concerned primarily with action. In *Hedda Gabler*, conversely, the unhappiness of the protagonist is indexed in terms of vocal tone as well as, on occasion, by means of body language. The directions *'impatiently'*, *'interrupting curtly'*, *'raising her arms and clenching her hands, as if in fury'*, and *'disturbed again'* (275–6) conduce to a sombre mood and contribute to the play's tragic impact overall. Vocal tone here is reinforced pictorially by the directions for setting, costume and lighting. A 'radical' text such as *Endgame* combines comic and serious elements but makes a distinct separation at the levels of form and content respectively. The play works to disorientate the spectator by the strategy of representing its bleak and uncompromising vision of the human condition by means of comic routine and savage humour.

We shall return to these various issues, and in particular to the implication of specific classes of direction for stage practice, in Chapter 7.

Part II
PERFORMANCE

6

SEMIOTICS OF PERFORMANCE

Where semiotics has provided a way of seeing the dramatic text which furthers our understanding of *how* the text is *made*, it has also provided the key to unlocking theatre from literature; the 'way to avoid imprisoning the theater in the text' (Kaisergruber 1977: 169). However, once the dramatic text is freed from the constraints of the traditional tools of literary criticism and from its consequent confinement to literature, and is considered in its theatrical context, the difficulties of 'reading' increase. The difficulties are created by what Barthes identified as the polysemic nature of theatre, i.e. its ability to draw on a number of sign-systems which do not operate in a linear mode but in a complex and simultaneously operating network unfolding in time and space.

Everything which is presented to the spectator within the theatrical frame is a sign, as the Prague School were the first to recognise. Reading signs is the way in which we set about making sense of the world. For example, we 'read' people we see in the street according to how they dress: scruffy hair, shabby outfit and ill-fitting shoes signify poverty; bowler hat, suit and umbrella signify city gent. Although we instinctively engage in such 'readings' because of our knowledge of dress codes (see Barthes 1968: 25–7), and act upon them accordingly, we have no way of knowing whether they are truly *meant*. This contrasts with theatre where everyone and everything placed within the theatrical frame has an artificial or pre-determined meaning. The process of signification is directed and controlled. Even if something has arbitrarily entered into the frame it is read as significant. In the 1988 Red Shift production of *The Misanthrope* the actor playing the lead had a bandaged hand, which invited a good deal of speculation by students seeing the performance as to possible meanings (externalisation of wounded heart? pride?), before the conclusion was drawn that it was simply an injury sustained by the actor and had no designated significance in terms of the theatrical event! (Recourse to the version used reveals a translator's direction for Alceste inadvertently to shatter the glass he is holding in the opening moments of the play (Bartlett 1990: 64–5), but this direction was not apparent in the performance in question.)

In twentieth-century traditions of Western theatre, the responsibility for organising the theatrical sign-system has fallen to the director. Whilst the dramatist is the originator of the linguistic sign-system, the director nowadays has control over the theatrical (as opposed to dramatic) shape and is faced with the task of organising the signifying systems of theatre at her/his disposal (lighting, scenery, props and so on) into a codified process appropriate to the production of a text. If the director fails in this task, then the performance will not make sense to the spectator. Trying to make sense of a badly organised sign-system can be a frustrating and unrewarding experience and is generally a sign of the artistic director's failure. Students who saw Shared Experience's production of *Nana*, adapted by Olwen Wymark, were initially unable to identify Nana, because the colour coding of the costumes gave prominence to a supporting character (Sabine, dressed in bright red finery) at the expense of the heroine (attired in the white undergarments which all the women in the cast used as a quick-changing base for multiple role-playing). Narrative confusion arose because the signification of the 'scarlet woman' was misplaced.

It is the responsibility of the director to ensure that the sign-systems operating in a production not only work in isolation, but also create the desired effect when combined with signs from other systems. Productions of plays in translation are often good examples of whether the theatrical sign-system has been carefully considered for clarity of meaning, because decisions have to be made about how to cross the sign-systems of two societies, languages, cultures and theatrical traditions. In the 1983 production of Dario Fo's *Can't Pay? Won't Pay!* by the Cambridge Theatre Company, the characters talked happily about spaghetti and macaroni, whilst they were seen with packets of Kellogg's Cornflakes. Either the director should have opted for signs of 'Italianicity' (see Barthes 1977: 33) or substituted their translation equivalents (e.g. potatoes or white sliced loaf for spaghetti).

The mixing of food signs in this example drew attention to the cross-cultural referencing, but to no significant purpose. Ideally, theatrical signs should combine (a) to transmit clear messages and (b) to hierarchise the messages sent. In the case of film, where semiotics has been widely adopted as a critical tool, the 'eye' of the camera helps to direct meaning. It selects the subject(s) to be viewed, thereby focusing our attention and directing the meaning-creating processes. In theatre, there is no such mediating device. Everything is put before us and we have a panoramic as opposed to a partial and pre-selected view of the stage. Signs operating within the theatrical frame need to be hierarchised in such a way as to help 'fix' meaning. Like language, theatre can foreground or 'make strange' specific elements of staging as a means to creating difference or significance. Types of theatre which operate self-referentially epitomise this process (see Chapter 2). Other types of theatre subvert the notion of a hierarchy of signs by offering a collage of signs which cannot be ordered or made sense of. Performance Art productions may, for example, offer a theatrical sign-system in chaos, where pleasure for the spectator relies on delighting in the experience of non-sense.

In general, where the audience is invited to make sense of what they see in a production, theatre draws on the elements of theatrical language at its disposal to establish a meaningful and hierarchised system of signification. Such a hierarchy is constantly shifting: a shipwreck may be signified by the use of lighting effects, its aftermath by soothing music, and its impact by the entrance of actors clothed in bedraggled costuming. Honzl's early essay on the 'Dynamics of the Sign in the Theater' was among the first statements to identify the 'changeability of the hierarchical scale of components of dramatic art' and to relate their links 'to the changeability of the theatrical sign' (1976 [1940]: 93; see also Chapter 1). Honzl's analysis demonstrated how different theatrical devices could be used to create the same sign – an actor can function as a scenic sign and designate a chair, lighting can signify a change in setting as opposed to scene-shifting, etc. – and how the hierarchy of devices changed according to the type of theatre.

101

This may seem obvious to us now, but it was precisely this form of early semiotic analysis which provided the touchstone for subsequent models of theatre language.

ACTOR AS SIGN

Whilst theatre operates as a sign-system through its changing use of theatrical components, the actor, throughout the history of theatre, has generally remained dominant in the shifting hierarchy. For this reason, the actor has proved an important subject of enquiry for semioticians:

> The most common case of the subject in the drama is the *figure of the actor*. The figure of the actor is the dynamic unity of an entire set of signs, the carrier of which may be the actor's body, voice, movements, but also various objects, from parts of the costume to the set. The important thing is, however, that the actor centers their meanings upon himself, and may do so to such an extent that by his actions he may replace all the sign carriers . . .
>
> (Veltruský 1964: 84)

We can address the complexity of the actor as a sign by separating out some of the key ways in which the sign of performer is constituted, by examining the actor as a public person, as the conveyor of the text, and as the site of interconnecting sign-systems.

In the first instance, the identity of a performer may make an important contribution to the process of signification. This is particularly true of actresses/actors who work within the tradition of the star system. A performer who has achieved fame and public recognition necessarily brings the sign of celebrity into play. Such a sign is constructed by various means of publicity: the promotion of a particular star image (e.g. Shakespearean actor, matinée idol), or through the less than desirable prurient promotion of a 'private' identity (whether fact or fiction). As Michael L. Quinn writes,

> Celebrity in its usual variety, though, is not composed of acting technique but of personal information. The first

requisite for celebrity is public notoriety, which is only sometimes achieved through acting. In the context of this public identity there then comes to exist a link between performer and audience, quite apart from the dramatic character . . .

(1990: 156)

For example, the identities of nineteenth-century star performers, who were fêted like the Hollywood stars of today, were important contributors to the construction of a stage image. Hence, the 'fact' that star actress Sarah Bernhardt was supposedly having an affair with her leading man at the Comédie Française contributed to the *femme fatale* image which encoded each of her performances and made her 'private' life a decodable sign within the theatrical frame. Association with a particular type of role also 'fixes' a star identity. Once Mrs Patrick Campbell had achieved overnight fame by playing Pinero's woman with a past in *The Second Mrs Tanqueray*, the image of fallen woman was henceforth encoded in Mrs Pat's on- and offstage identity, a confusion of role and reality (see Campbell 1922: 82). Conversely, the actress Ellen Terry, in reality an unmarried mother with two children, managed to acquire a star reputation as one of the most respected and respectable performers in Victorian and Edwardian theatre.

A star performer might also be a sign of a particular school of acting. Note the case of stars whose names become synonymous with an acting style or tradition: for example, the equation of the nineteenth-century French actor, Constant Coquelin, with the anti-emotionalist theory of acting. Or, to take a modern example, who can see Brando without thinking 'method acting'? In short, it is absurd to think of the actor as an empty sign. As Elam aptly expresses it, 'actors may be more than empty vessels waiting to contain the dramatist's fine illocutionary wine' (1988: 46), and in the field of theatre semiotics there is still space for detailed study of stars as signs, of the kind Richard Dyer offered for film studies (see Dyer 1979; the introduction to Quinn 1990 promises more detailed work on the 'stage figure in different theatrical contexts').

In contrast, there are other styles of performance, notably ensemble-based theatre, which resist the celebrity syndrome and performer–role identification, and the currency of the

103

actor as sign changes in consequence. Brecht's concept of the performer having a social function, the performer as 'demonstrator', offers an example in which what is shown is more important than the individual who shows it. Hence, groups performing within the Brechtian tradition engage in multiple role-playing which resists the actor–character identification of the star system. This challenges both the actor and the spectator to deny the gravitation towards the instinctive interest in the mimetic sign – human beings playing other human beings.

While certain schools of theory attribute special functions to the actor, as in the instance of Brecht's notion of the social function of the actor, the performer's dominant function is that of speaking the dramatic text. The actor functions as a link between the dramatic and the theatrical; 'the problematic of the actor is a problematic in double time: – dramaturgic time – scenographic time. . . . Through the spoken word of the actor, the writing progresses from one of the loci of writing to another . . .' (Gourville 1977: 121). 'The craft of the actor', as Gourville goes on to explain, 'consists in the fluctuation between the two loci of the writing'; of synthesising the director's scripting of the stage and the writer's scripting of the text. The two 'texts' are interdependent:

> What we have, then, is a relationship of mutual and shifting constraints between two kinds of text, neither of which is prior and neither of which is precisely 'immanent' within the other, since each text is radically transformed by its relations with the other (the written text, for example, ceases to be written within the domain of the performance text, and the non-linguistic elements of the performance text are not 'present' within the written text but remain as mere memories or potentialities).
>
> (Elam 1977: 160)

Semioticians have therefore overcome the problems of arguing about the supremacy of text or performance, and looked to overlap rather than to difference.

We could usefully extend Elam's point in relation to the actor by returning to Ingarden's distinction between *Haupttext* and *Nebentext*. The transformation to which Elam refers is sited principally in the actor's task of speaking the written or *Haupttext* and realising the potential of the *Nebentext*. Whereas these two 'texts' are clearly differentiated in the dramatic script, in performance the two are synthesised into a *density* of signs' which generate largely from the actor, and it is in this sense that we can refer to the performer as a locus of multiple interconnecting sign-systems.

ACTOR AND CLASSIFICATION OF SIGN-SYSTEMS

Tadeusz Kowzan's early attempt to classify the sign-systems of theatre (as cited in Chapter 1) highlighted the centrality of the actor to the thirteen systems he identified (1968: 73, also cited in Kowzan's subsequent and full-length study, 1975). The classification is reproduced here as Table 6.1.

Table 6.1 Kowzan's classification of sign-systems

Signs	Sub-group	Actor grouping	Auditive/Visual	Space/Time	Sign type
1 Word 2 Tone	Spoken text	Actor	Auditive signs	Time	Auditive signs (actor)
3 Mime 4 Gesture 5 Movement	Expression of the body	Actor	Visual signs	Space and time	Visual signs (actor)
6 Make-up 7 Hair-style 8 Costume	Actor's external appearance	Actor	Visual signs	Space	Visual signs (actor)
9 Properties 10 Settings 11 Lighting	Appearance of the stage	Outside the actor	Visual signs	Space and time	Visual signs (outside the actor)
12 Music 13 Sound effects	Inarticulate sounds	Outside the actor	Auditive signs	Time	Auditive signs (outside the actor)

The eight groups with which Kowzan heads his taxonomy relate directly to the actor as opposed to the five which he classifies as 'outside the actor'. By using the distinction between

105

auditive and visual signs, Kowzan establishes four larger groups of signs, distinguishing between the auditive and visual signs generated by the actor and the auditive and visual signs generated by systems outside the actor. The actor is therefore shown to be a site for the transmission of auditive signs relating to text (which extends Elam's point), and as a principal site of visual signification.

Kowzan's preliminary attempts to classify the sign-systems of theatre and his isolation of the actor as the central signifying locus, may be illustrated by means of a practical example. Act II of *Phaedra* was chosen by Sarah Bernhardt for her first London performance in 1879, and the scene from the act which attracted most comment from the drama critics was scene five: the climactic confrontation between Phaedra and Hippolytus. From accounts of the performance, we can reconstruct the auditive and visual signs of the actor according to Kowzan's system.

Analysing the performer as a locus of sign-systems, as demonstrated in Table 6.2, serves to show how the impressionistic reading of Bernhardt's Phaedra, as a woman overtaken by passion, is arrived at. How the text is spoken affects the foregrounding of meaning. Stress patterns, intonation, volume and so on, all contribute to a specific 'reading' (on stress and speaking the text, see Barker 1977: Ch. 14). Equally, the external appearance and movement of the performer extend the textual reading. For example, Bernhardt's baring of the breast and seizing of the sword are signified in the text (see lines 704 and 711), and are there to be brought out in performance if the actress chooses (for reinforcement of this point, see Chapters 5 and 7).

The deployment of certain signs and the exclusion of others constitutes an 'interpretation' of the role directed by the performer (the role of the director as master of spectacle had yet to arrive). An alternative 'interpretation' might have hierarchised signs of the majestic, of a queenly as opposed to womanly passion, a violent as opposed to feminine abandonment. This was in fact the way Bernhardt's predecessor, Félix Rachel, had played the role earlier in the century. Rachel selected those auditive and visual signs which would foreground the majesty, restraint, grandeur and ferocity of a woman poisoned by a passion inflicted on her by the gods. In consequence,

Table 6.2 Kowzan's sign-system in practice

System	Signs	Signification
1. Word	Alexandrine verse	'Artistic language' French classical tragedy, etc.
2. Tone	Delivery: *prestissimo*	Passion
	Stress: lines running together, individual words not stressed	Lyricism
	Volume: *pianissimo*	Femininity/seduction
	Timbre: strained	Intensity
3. Mime	Facial acting	Despair, self-loathing, guilt, passion, etc.
4. Gesture	Arms open	Declaration of love
	Arms clinging	Pleading
	Baring of breast	Death wish
	Seizing of sword	Death wish intensified
5. Movement	Away from Hippolytus	Self-loathing/disgust
	Towards Hippolytus	Passion/self-abandonment
	General mode: writhing, febrile, agitated, serpentine	Despair, self-loathing, guilt, passion, etc. Seduction/femininity
6. Make-up	Ashen, eyes and lips accentuated	Distressed beauty
7. Hair-style	Dishevelled, unruly	Abandonment
8. Costume	White drapery	Classicism, femininity, delicacy

she constructed a rendition quite different from Bernhardt's feminine, seductive and womanly victim.

Once a preliminary identification of signs is established, the complexity and problematics of analysis begin to appear. Where, for example, do we classify those signs which are in some sense 'natural' but which operate as directed meanings in the performance context? The physical attributes of a performer are natural or given, but acquire significance on the stage (to wit, the semitic signs of Bernhardt's features, her long thin arms and slight body which signified frailty). Alternatively an actor may be suffering uncontrollably from nerves and these in turn become 'directed' signs in the system. (On the occasion of the performance described, Bernhardt was suffering both from fatigue and stage fright, which multiplied the signs of world-weariness or agitation.) Where – in relation to Sarah Bernhardt, the great French actress, society figure, rule-breaker and *femme fatale* – do we classify performer identity? Equally there is no space to classify those signs which, if we look beyond the actor for a moment, are generated by the audience. Signs of anxiety (hushed auditorium, breathless spectating), and of relief after the passionate outburst (thunderous applause), were recorded as interacting with Bernhardt's performance. Her pitch of frenzy, intensity and passion were in turn affected by audience response. Such questions point to the difficulty of classifying the sign-systems, queries which we raise as observations rather than criticisms of Kowzan's system, which was offered as a rudimentary exploration, and which has historically proved an important taxonomy in furthering semiotic analysis of theatre, its limitations notwithstanding. The questioning also points to an ever-present difficulty for the student of theatre – the sense that no two performances are the same. Despite controlled direction of the relatively static sign-systems (see discussion of settings in Chapter 8), fluid components, such as audience reaction or mood of the actor, can both change the reception processes and alter the levels of signification, from performance to performance.

THE PAVIS QUESTIONNAIRE

Further taxonomies have followed in the wake of Kowzan's pioneering classification, addressed primarily to the student of theatre as aids to performance analysis. (Kowzan worked on theatre as a sign-system with his own students at the University of Lyon and published a volume on their semiotic readings of productions. See Kowzan 1976.) Esslin's taxonomy in *The Field of Drama* increases Kowzan's thirteen sign-systems to twenty-two and offers a further ten which extend to cinematic media alone (1987: 103–5). It usefully builds in categories related to 'framing systems outside the drama proper' (e.g. architecture, publicity) which Kowzan's system does not take account of. However, Kowzan's classification of sign-systems and their possible auditive and visual configurations is a far more useful framing device than Esslin's linear classification, which, for example, unhelpfully classifies music and non-musical sounds under 'Aural signs', whilst identifying delivery of text (also an auditive sign) under 'Sign systems at the actor's disposal'. Furthermore, there is no space within Esslin's system for accounting for the spectator's role in the production of meaning.

Far more useful in this respect, in terms of both accessibility and comprehensiveness, is the 1985 Pavis Questionnaire (see Table 6.3). The questionnaire was designed for students of theatre without a background in semiotics and provides a useful framing device for performance analysis, one which can 'be used as a checklist (even an "idiot's guide") for the study of performance' (Pavis 1985a: 209–10). Its usefulness lies in its listing of theatrical sign-systems, the basic 'what to look for' approach, but it also guides the student from identification to an analysis of signification by virtue of the sub-questioning/discussion points offered within the categories. It constantly addresses the question of 'how' meaning is constructed and creates the possibility of guiding the student from the 'how' to the 'why'. For example, under category nine, consideration of 'what kind of dramaturgical choices have been made' invites the student to move from a fundamental grasp of *how* formal strategies work in a production to an analysis of purpose or ideological intent underlying the dramaturgical choices. The opening category of general discussion offers a way of putting the student at ease, whilst also eliciting immediate reactions which can then be pursued and analytically shaped through subsequent questioning. Similarly, later categories (12, 13, and 14) return to the question of what worked or did not work, in a way which helps to synthesise those initial reactions into a reasoned and informed response. Though a consequence of this may be to invite duplication or repetition (Pavis himself cites the 'unavoidable overlaps in formulating the answers'), the student's response will probably be more thoroughly and analytically formulated as a result. One likely outcome of this approach is enquiry into how sign-systems are combined and hierarchised to create a density of meaning.

SIGNS AND CODES

Theatre semioticians in the wake of Kowzan's taxonomy and subsequent classifications have focused not only on the systems of signs, but on the processes of codification involved in such systems. In respect of this point, Elam's distinction

Table 6.3 Parvis questionnaire

1. *General discussion of performance*
(a) what holds elements of performance together
(b) relationship between systems of staging
(c) Coherence or incoherence
(d) aesthetic principles of the production
(e) what do you find disturbing about the production; strong moments or weak, boring moments

2. *Scenography*
(a) spatial forms: urban, architectural, scenic, gestural, etc.
(b) relationship between audience space and acting space
(c) system of colours and their connotations
(d) principles of organisation of space
– relationship between on-stage and off-stage
– links between space utilised and fiction of the staged dramatic text

3. *Lighting system*

4. *Stage properties*
type, function, relationship to space and actors' bodies

5. *Costumes*
how they work; relationship to actors' bodies

6. *Actors' performances*
(a) individual or conventional style of acting
(b) relation between actor and group
(c) relation between text and body, between actor and role

(d) quality of gestures and mime
(e) quality of voices
(f) how dialogues develop

7. *Function of music and sound effects*

8. *Pace of performance*
(a) overall pace
(b) pace of certain signifying systems (lighting,. costumes, gestures, etc.)
(c) steady or broken pace

9. *Interpretation of story-line in performance*
(a) what story is being told
(b) what kind of dramaturgical choices have been made
(c) what are ambiguities in performance and what are points of explanation
(d) how is plot structured
(e) how is story constructed by actors and staging
(f) what is genre of dramatic text

10. *Text in performance*
(a) main features of translation
(b) what role is given to dramatic text in production
(c) relationship between text and image

11. *Audience*
(a) where does performance take place
(b) what expectations did you have of performance
(c) how did audience react
(d) role of spectator in production of meaning

Table 6.3 Continued

---

12. *How to notate (photograph and film) this production*
(a) how to notate performance technically
(b) which images have you retained

13. *What cannot be put into signs*
(a) what did not make sense in your interpretation of the production

(b) what was not reducible to signs and meaning (and why)

14.
(a) Are there any special problems that need examining
(b) Any comments, suggestions for further categories for the questionnaire and the production

---

between *theatrical* codes and *dramatic* codes is particularly useful (1980: 52). Where code is understood as 'an ensemble of *correlational* rules governing the formation of sign-relationships' (ibid.: 50), so theatrical codes appertain to the correlational ensemble encoded in a particular performance (hence taking on board the notion of each performance as a unique and unrepeatable experience) and dramatic codes apply to the conventions of drama, e.g. generic, structural, stylistic (ibid.). Elam further articulates these codes as sub-codes because theatre is 'parasitic' on the cultural codes which operate in the real world (for full details, see Elam's table: 57–62). Theatre establishes its network of codified sign-systems by virtue of the cultural codes which govern behaviour, speech, dress, make-up, etc., in society at large. In the Bernhardt example, decoding the sign-system would need to take account of behavioural codes in relation to the dramatic sub-coding of rules governing tragic roles and the theatrical sub-coding appertaining to the histrionic style.

Among the systems of codes, two in particular have attracted the attention of theatre semioticians: *proxemics* (codes governing the use of space) and *kinesics* (codes governing movement).

SPATIAL CODES

In the shift from script and the reader to script and the spectator, the act of reading, located in time, is transformed into the act of spectating which takes place in time and space. Because drama (as opposed to poetry and fiction) requires the dimensions of space and time, the means by which it unfolds and takes its shape in these two dimensions constitutes an important consideration in the analysis of the theatrical context. Hence, theatre semioticians are concerned with understanding the organisation of space, and the ways in which spatial codes are used to generate meaning. Use has been made of the studies of *proxemics*, i.e. the human use of space, carried out by anthropologists. Such studies have looked at how we organise our living space in terms of both the private (the houses we build and choose to live in, etc.) and the public (architecture and organisation of the workplace, etc.). Theatre draws 'parasitically' on these behavioural codes in relation to space, to the extent that they serve as an important dynamic in organising and creating the boundaries between spectator and performer. This in turn influences the production of meaning in a performance context.

How theatre organises its space has changed throughout its history, conditioned by the evolution of cultural, societal, political, pecuniary or performance factors. Why and how this happens is a complex question relating to the interaction of theatre and society in different ages. The use of spatial codes within theatre needs to take account both of the diachronic (the historical evolution of the space) and the synchronic (organisation of the space within a particular period) in terms of architecture, staging, and configurations of actor(s) and spectator(s).

Architecture

Building for theatre means giving theatre its *own space*. Marking out a space specifically, if not exclusively, for theatre means establishing a space which is relatively fixed. The style in which it is designed and built is in itself a cultural sign both of theatre and the society which creates it. For example, the boom in theatre building in the Victorian and Edwardian periods with its opulence, and lavish, ornate styles, was a sign of the commercial orientation of theatre and a celebration of middle-class wealth, prosperity and stability.

Not all theatre takes its own space, and where theatre carries the function of being a part of, rather than apart from, life, then spatial boundaries tend to be less formal, less fixed. Greek theatre, it would appear, began in non-theatre-designated spaces. Performance in the towns possibly took place in the *agora* (market place). In the villages, use was made of any open space, such as a threshing floor, to stage these early, ceremonial rituals in which most or all of the community took part (see Leacroft and Leacroft 1984: 2). From the informal act of watching in a participatory mode developed the act of watching in a contemplative mode, and of marking out a formal space for spectating, as reflected in the evolution of the sophisticated, horseshoe-shaped amphitheatres. The architectural development gives credence to scholars of Greek theatre who locate its origins in the shift from ritual to drama; from the acting out of a rain dance to water the crops to watching the rain dance as a performance (see Harrison 1951), where the latter marks out a space for the performers and the spectators.

Similarly, medieval theatre in England moves from its ceremonial base within the church, where the spectator is also an actant in the ceremony, to outside performances on pageant wagons for example, where boundaries between spectator and actor were both defined (in terms of the wagon-stage) and fluid (actors would leap down and mingle with the street audience).

With the notion of a relatively fixed architectural structure comes the notion of sectioning the spectator's space; of hierarchising according to status and/or wealth. This was true of Greek theatre as it developed, where, for example, front-row benches (*prohedria*) were reserved for the priests and dignitaries. This phenomenon may also be traced in the history of English theatre which gradually hierarchised the seating of the audience in relation to class and the ability to pay, eventually forcing the groundlings out of the pit and into the gods (see Leacroft and Leacroft 1984: 58). This trend was to reach its apotheosis in the bourgeois theatre of the last century which, in design and function, worked towards excluding all but the wealthier classes. This goes hand in hand with the erosion of the traditional, social function of the theatre and the location of theatre spaces within the community, in favour of indoor playhouses wherein the picture-framing of the theatrical event holds up a mirror to an elite sector of society for passive and reaffirmative viewing.

Trends in twentieth-century theatre have demonstrated a reaction against this, and witnessed a move away from the fixed, architectural theatre space, and the popularising of the notion of appropriating, on an *ad hoc* basis, spaces in which to make theatre – the ability, as Peter Brook describes it, to 'take any empty space and call it a bare stage' (1968: 11). The unfixing of the boundaries between the spectating space and the performing space reflects an attempt to be inclusive, i.e. to establish an active mode in the contract between performer and spectator.

Spaces within spaces

Whether performing in a designated theatre space or finding an 'empty space', whichever tradition has dictated, altering the *proxemic* relations between audience space and playing space remains feasible. This is particularly true of the bourgeois and modern periods, where the deployment of lighting means that a space can be created within a space. The introduction of lighting established the convention of the darkened auditorium (a further means of marking out the performance and spectating areas), and limited the spectator's spatial awareness to the stage area; a radically different spatial awareness to that of the open-air, daylight theatres of previous ages. The creative use of lighting means that an intimate space can be created within the confines of a large and inflexible venue.

Similarly, the shape of a playing space can be altered by means of set construction. In current theatre, many companies operate as middle- or small-scale touring groups, without a building base of their own, and of necessity require flexible sets which have to adapt to any number of fixed spaces. Modern productions of plays from earlier periods sometimes aim to rebuild the theatre space of that period within the modern playhouse. Several of the productions by the Medieval Players, for example, were staged on a pageant-wagon, which redefined the stage space in which it was set. The Barbican's Pit was reshaped for Deborah Warner's 1989 production of Sophocles' *Electra* into a Greek-style auditorium, which situated the audience on tiered seating in a fan shape around the playing arena.

Given the nineteenth-century legacy of spaces with fixed boundaries, the transformation of the audience space is a more difficult proposition, unless the performance takes place in a studio space with flexible seating arrangements. Certain styles of theatre have challenged this, either by having the actors invade the audience space or by inviting the audience on to the stages. Where this is a recognised convention (e.g. inviting audience members on stage in a pantomime), the boundaries of space do not disorientate. Other styles of theatre, such as Arrabal's Theatre of Panic (which advocated the use of revolving seats for the audience in order to surround them with the stage action), are potentially more threatening and disruptive in terms of breaking the spectator–performer spatial contract.

Actor–spectator Configurations

Not only do spatial codes set out to define, shape and construct the meaning of the spectating and playing spaces, they also govern relations between performers on the stage, and performer–spectator interactions.

How actors arrange and present themselves on stage is important in directing and focusing the spectator's attention. Spatial arrangements between actors are important indicators of identity, status, relationships and centrality to action (a point pursued in Chapter 7). Again, such configurations are governed by the practical conditions of space and the dramatic and theatrical codes governing its use. An intimate scene in Greek theatre, for example, would be intimate relative to the scale and sheer size of the theatre, requiring a greater proxemic distance between actors to signify intimacy than that of a love scene played on the nineteenth-century, picture-frame stage.

Variations in the proxemic relation between the actor and the spectator can radically alter the spectator's perception and reception of a production. Poor sight lines, or other restrictions, can mar a whole production. Being seated on the front row for a production can create an intimacy with the performer which is not shared by someone seated at the back of the auditorium. Likewise, spatial relations between spectator and spectator also condition our viewing and inform our 'reading' of a production. The public, shared experience of collective spectating is radically different from private, isolated television viewing in one's home.

READING THE BODY: KINESICS

Whilst configurations of actors within a space constitute a codified method of generating meaning, so too do the movements of actors within the space. Studies of the human body as a means of communication, i.e. *kinesics*, have also been used by theatre semioticians to analyse and codify gesture in performance. The task is an extremely complex and difficult one: 'nothing is easier for the critic or for the spectator than to refer to the text; nothing is more difficult, on the other hand, than to capture the slightest gesture of the actor' (Pavis 1981a: 65). Kowzan's categories of mime, gesture and movement, grouped under 'expression of the body', locate a primary level of difficulty. In performance, these are systems which operate in a simultaneous flow throughout. For students of film, the use of editing or video equipment means that a filmed sequence can be cut up into a series of stills, and sequences of action/movement studied. But the spectator in theatre is faced with the task of reading the body/face in a constant state of flux and action. Furthermore, as Pavis comments, 'Once gesture becomes the object of a descriptive discourse, it loses all specificity; reduced to the level of a text, it does not give any account of its volume, of its signifying force, of its place in the global stage message' (1981a: 65).

Despite these levels of difficulty, reading the body is a task which the theatre semiotician must face up to, given its centrality to the theatrical sign-system and the production of meaning. Just as the mode of dramatic dialogue is essentially deictic, so too is the use of the body in theatrical communication: 'deictic gesture, indicating the actor and his relations to the stage, is of decisive importance to theatrical performance, being the primary means whereby the presence and the spatial orientations of the body are established' (Elam 1980: 72). In performance, establishing the 'I am here in this space' is achieved both by verbal and gestural *deixis*. In speaking the dialogue, the actor is also using the body to point to her/his relation to the on-stage dramatic world, her/his action within it.

116

Speaking the text involves speaking with the body. Whenever we converse, facial expressions, gestures of the hand, and so on, come into play. Use of body language helps to fix the meaning of an utterance: 'Yes' accompanied by a nod of the head, reinforces signification of assent. Or, alternatively, it can 'unfix' meaning and further ambiguity: 'Yes' accompanied by a shake of the head. It may even be used as a substitute for speech: a nod of the head says 'Yes'. It is through the use of gesture that intention and attitude are commonly marked out in dramatic performance (for a detailed discussion, see Elam 1980: 73–8), though the nature and type of gesture, whilst drawing on the kinesics of the body, is further conditioned and codified by dramatic and theatrical conventions.

History of acting and gesture

Whilst decoding gesture presents a difficult area in terms of performance analysis, organising preliminary thoughts towards a semiotics of theatrical gesture is aided by linking the use of dramatic gesture to the history of acting and the theories which surround it. Again use will be made of the three-phase developmental model.

Theatre which signposts the actor and her/his dramatic world reveals a dominant use of deictic gesture. The intra-dialogic directions in *Oedipus the King* are predominantly markers of deictic gesture (e.g. 'The men over there/are signalling – Creon's just arriving': 162). Here, gesture is used as a means of drawing attention to the dramatic world, its characters and action, of 'pointing to' a world which it establishes through artifice, distance and convention. Moreover, the hierarchisation of plot/action over character (see Aristotle 1965: 39) prioritises the 'doing', the 'acting out' of events and resists character development and identification.

The use of deictic gesture predominates in this first phase of theatre, where the actor functions as a sign of the actor and distance between actor and role is established. The emblematic mode of *Everyman* is essentially one of 'showing' or 'pointing to' (e.g. 'DEATH: *Everyman* stand still; whither art though going/Thus gaily? . . . I will show you/. . . That will I show thee . . .' 209). Entrances and exits are deictically marked in *As You Like It* as they are in *Oedipus the King* and require appropriate gestures to signal arrivals and departures (e.g. 'ADAM. Yonder comes my master, your brother.' I.1.26/'CELIA. Yonder sure they are coming. Let us now stay and see it.' I.2.137). Such intra-dialogic directions map out both stage proxemics and body movement and consciously signal gesture, movement and actor configurations to the spectator.

The duality between actor and role, clearly marked in this first phase of drama, is not challenged until the eighteenth century, when the emotionalist versus anti-emotionalist debate begins. This was advanced by the publication of Diderot's *The Paradox of Acting* (1957 [1830]), and continues to be argued today (for example in debates around the methodologies of Stanislavsky and Brecht). In essence, the debate centres on whether the actor aims for complete identification with character, or whether a duality/distance between the actor and her/his role arises due to technique and the 'art of acting'. Examples of both approaches are manifest in the 'bourgeois' century, and tend to be linked to theatrical form. Types of theatre which were formulaic in construction and which prioritised action over character, such as the well-made play or melodrama, encouraged distance. In terms of body movement, this encouraged the use of 'picture acting', where emotional states were signified by a gestural picture governed by clearly codified rules. In the melodrama, *Lady Audley's Secret*, the eponymous 'heroine's' final state of madness is announced by herself accompanied by wild laughter and a gesture to the temples to signify the madness in her head, followed by an on-stage death and 'tableau of sympathy'. There is no psychology of madness; the state is announced and visually represented through gesture. Even in the great advocates of emotionalist or histrionic acting, like Sarah Bernhardt, acting styles revealed a recourse to technique and the representation of emotional states through gestural picture. In the wake of Ibsen and the 'New Drama', however, emphasis on character and character psychology demanded a different response in acting styles. Actors sought a closer identification with character as they struggled to understand or come to terms with a role: 'It was not until Ibsen, Stanislavsky, and their successors that the term "action", so closely associated with "gesture" over the years, gradually evolved to mean "motivation"' (Cima 1983: 13). For a nineteenth-century actress playing Hedda, recourse to codified gesture to externalise an inner state was inappropriate and instigated a demand for a new style and a change in performance *kinesics* centred on motivation:

> With the advent of Ibsen's plays and their individual-ized characters, however, a revised category of gestures became necessary: the *autistic gesture*, or subtle visual sign of the character's soliloquy with himself. It is this type of introspective gesture which allowed the Ibsen actress to show the audience the dialogue taking place within the character and the various lines of action she had to convey. Often the actress gestured through subtle facial expressions, especially eye and lip movements, or through the movement of hands to the body, such as, possibly, the frenzied movement of Hedda's hands when she is left alone after Miss Tesman's exit.
>
> (Cima 1983: 22)

In the modern period, theatre which adheres to the illusionist concerns of the previous century espouses character motiva-tion and a use of gesture which aims to mimic or reproduce life. Plays and performances which share modernist concerns, however, seek to disrupt the mimetic patterning of speech and gesture. Brecht's theory of *gestic* acting advocates a kinesic mode which is interrogative, in which the actor uses her/his body as a site for the simultaneous questioning of the world she/he demonstrates within the dramatic fiction. Modernist styles which have incorporated eastern traditions of theatre look to ways of demoting or abolishing *logos* in favour of a physical language (see, e.g., Artaud 1974). Beckett's work has increasingly divorced speech from physical movement: through the technique of the splintered couple, one who moves and one who talks (e.g. Clov and Hamm), the absence of speech (e.g. Clov's mime, or *Act Without Words: A Mime for one Player*), or the absence of body movement (e.g. the half-buried Winnie in Act I of *Happy Days*).

Current concerns of women's theatre and notions of 'writing the body' in performance may, in time, yield fruitful investi-gations for a semiotics of theatrical gesture. Projects like the Cardiff-based *Magdalena*, which work with body and voice and a visual style of theatre to examine the possibilities (or impos-sibilities) of a 'female language' of theatre, begin with an idea of

119

what is to be rejected: i.e., the rejection of theatrical tradition which constructs the 'female as sign' (see Ferris 1990). Patterns of speech and movement which define the 'female' in male terms give way, once refused, to the possibility of an anarchic, liberating and self-defining process for the female performer. The stage of kinesic rejection, the revolt of the female body, is to be seen, for example, at the climax of Churchill's dinner tableau in *Top Girls*, where 'NIJO is laughing and crying. JOAN gets up and is sick in a corner. MARLENE is drinking ISABELLA'S brandy' (29).

SPECTATOR AND THE PRODUCTION OF MEANING

Given the premise that theatre operates as a sign-system, as a system which sends out signs or messages, the receiver of the signs also merits consideration within the theatrical frame. Classifications of sign-systems have tended to leave the spectator out of the frame, as was demonstrated previously, though Pavis's invitation to performance analysis quite rightly invites consideration of the 'role of the spectator' in the 'production of meaning' (Pavis 1985a). This serious omission perhaps reflects a dominant trend in current mainstream theatre which, by virtue of its unquestioning and reaffirmative nature, reduces the spectator to a passive recipient of signs and does not demand an interactive or active role in the production of meaning. West End or Broadway theatre thrives on a staple diet of such entertainment, requiring the spectator to consume, rather than think. The consequence of this reduction of the role of the spectator is an unproductive erosion of the traditional communicative function of theatre.

Quite clearly, although theatre offers a system of signs which have been artificially placed and purposively thought out to create meaning, levels of interpretation must vary between individual spectators. Just as Barthes identified the 'non-innocent' reader (see Barthes 1975: 10), so theatre is attended by the 'non-innocent' spectator whose world view, cultural understanding or placement, class and gender condition and shape her/his response. Furthermore, before we even purchase a ticket for a performance (the sign of a contract between actor and spectator) our expectations of the theatrical event may already have been shaped by pre-publicity, location of venue, knowledge of the text, critical reviews, judgements of friends who have been to see it. All of these factors have a possible bearing on how we shape a meaning from the production.

More recent studies within the ambit of theatre semiotics have attempted to redress the previous imbalance; to shift the early semiotic focus on the actor to the spectator. Pavis, writing in 1988, comments:

> It has now been understood and accepted that staging is not the mere physical uttering of a text with the appropriate intonation so that all can grasp the correct meaning; it is creating contexts of utterance in which the exchanges between verbal and nonverbal elements can take place. The utterance is always intended for an audience, with the result that mise en scène can no longer ignore the spectator and must even include him or her as the receptive pole in a circuit between the mise en scène produced by artists and the hypotheses of the spectators, artistically involved themselves in the mise en scène.
>
> (99–100)

In the same collection of essays, Elam documents thoughts around the 'perlocutionary act' of theatre, the 'doing things to the audience', tabulating theoretical positions and the perlocutionary effects they aspire to, both in terms of the end result and the means to achieving that end (1988: 52–3). Hence, the gestic acting of Brecht's Epic Theatre is designed to raise social awareness *en route* to taking revolutionary action, whereas the Aristotelian 'perlocutionary model' invites the purgation of excess pity and fear (and, by extension, offers a benevolent and reaffirming world view). Furthermore, Elam makes a plea for semiotics to embrace the '*punctum*, or *pathos*, or if you like audience passion, that compulsion which . . . motivates the receiver's active participation in the artistic practice', an experience which it has hitherto excluded (Elam 1988: 49). It is precisely this exclusion of 'audience passion' from studies of theatre semiotics that has generated a suspicion of its mode of enquiry as reductive, scientific, or somehow inappropriate to the nature of theatre. Perhaps the exclusion, as Elam suggests, is again symptomatic of our staple diet of theatrical fare in which 'passion' is significant by its absence. For those rare occasions in which it does arise, a semiotics of theatre needs to make space for its inclusion and write the spectator into the frame as an engaged, active receiver.

We shall return to the role of the spectator in Chapter 8.

7

STAGE DIRECTIONS II

In Chapter 5 we attempted a systematic analysis of the nature and functions of stage directions. Our findings were recorded as a tabular classification of intra- and extra-dialogic directions under six headings: the identification, and physical and vocal definition of character; formal conventions of speech; design elements; technical elements. Whereas that analysis was pitched at the level of text, we propose now to examine the implications of the directions, as a sign-system operative in parallel to the dialogue, for stage practice. We are concerned here with the current adequacy of stage directions, their status and their relevance to performance and production, rather than with issues of historical significance. Hence we shall address the functions of directions within the theatrical context, considering in turn their bearing on the work of the actor, the designer and lighting designer, and the technician, and on that of the director in her/his orchestration of the production overall.

STATUS OF STAGE DIRECTIONS

The issue of the status of stage directions is subject to contestation both among semioticians and within the theatrical profession. In the 'classic' text, the preponderantly intra-dialogic directions serve both to inform the production in the course of the rehearsal process and, subsequently, to engage the spectator in acts of imaginative participation. In the 'bourgeois' and in the 'radical' text, the intra-dialogic directions are supplemented (and, in some categories, replaced) by the extra-dialogic. In contradistinction to the 'classic' text, where such information as is conveyed intra-dialogically with regard to staging is communicated directly to the spectator in the course of the performance, in the 'bourgeois' and the 'radical' text the probability is that comparable information will be located in extra-dialogic directions, and that it will in consequence be communicated to the spectator only to the extent to which it is translated into a *mise-en-scène*.

What, then, is at stake when the dramatist's suggestions for staging are not incorporated into the director's *mise-en-scène*? Critical opinion is divided as to the usefulness of stage directions, in particular the more 'visible' extra-dialogic mode. Elam and Pavis, for example, share the view that directions constitute for the dramatist a means of asserting authorial control over the processes whereby the text is realised in performance. Arguing against Searle, Elam complains at the 'apotheosis' of the extra-dialogic directions as the 'real communicational substance of the text', and therefore at what he takes to be the concomitant marginalisation of the dialogue (1988: 44–5). Pavis suggests that the textual status of extra-dialogic directions is 'uncertain', and that the director is therefore relieved of the obligation of adhering to them. With regard to dialogue, he observes that 'stage directions concerning the circumstances of utterances are not the ultimate truth of the text, a formal command to produce the text in such a manner, or even an indispensable shifter between text and performance' (1988: 89). Where Elam appears to wish to save the dramatist from her/himself, Pavis is concerned to privilege the autonomy of the director at the expense of the dramatist and, in all probability, of the text in performance. Issacharoff, while agreeing that 'performance undermines the notion of the text as the repository of stable meanings' (1988: 139), recognises the stage directions as 'potential speech acts', i.e. as a non-verbal metadiscourse (when translated into a *mise-en-scène*) which functions to enable the verbal discourse (dialogue) to 'speak'. Hence, he is led to ask whether directions should be rejected out of hand, as is proposed by Elam and Pavis. His own view, demonstrated in the course of an analysis of the codes of radio drama is that 'stage directions can be seen as one of the major forces contributing to the cohesion of the dramatic script' (ibid.: 5).

We noted in Chapter 5 the emergence of the extra-dialogic mode of direction as a concomitant of the development of illusionistic theatre in the modern period. The craft of the dramatist is extended to take cognisance, for example, of the stage environment which the characters inhabit, and of their physical interaction within that space. What is recorded, in the form of the extra-dialogic directions, is what the dramatist 'sees' and 'hears' as s/he composes stage picture and dialogue. If, in the context of theatrical practice, it is less than necessary to accord canonical status to stage directions, it is equally unproductive to reject them on a principle of directorial autonomy. At the very least, it is in the interest of the director and her/his collaborators to regard the directions as adjuncts to the dialogue, and to investigate seriously and systematically their potential usefulness to the production in process. We shall pursue this issue further, in relation to the visual dimension of theatre, in Chapter 8.

Table 5.1 identifies and illustrates, in both the intra- and extra-dialogic modes, fifty-seven varieties of stage direction. Of these, thirty-five relate to character, and are thus addressed to the actor; thirteen are concerned with setting and with the lighting of the set, and are addressed to the designer and lighting designer; nine deal with lighting and sound effects, and are addressed to the technician. These broad categories are not, of course, exclusive. The actor, for example, may be supposed to take some interest in the design elements, at least in so far as these have a bearing on the character to be played. And an overview of all aspects of performance and production is a prerequisite for the effective exercise of the director's function. In the sections which follow, we shall offer a detailed analysis of representative sets of extra-dialogic stage directions in terms of the categories noted above.

THE ACTOR

The primary theatrical function of the actor is the representation of character. Information on the appearance, behaviour and interplay of character in the post-'classic' text is conventionally furnished, whether explicitly or implicitly, by the extra-dialogic directions. In *Hedda Gabler*, two characters, Hedda and Mrs Elvsted, are identified and described at their respective first entrances by virtually parallel formulations.

125

HEDDA	MRS ELVSTED
1. HEDDA . . . *is a woman of twenty-nine.*	*She is a couple of years younger than* HEDDA.
2. *Her face and figure show breeding and distinction, her complexion has an even pallor.*	MRS ELVSTED *is a slender little thing with pretty, soft features.*
3. *Her eyes are steel-grey; cold, clear and calm.*	*Her eyes are light blue, large, round and slightly prominent, with a startled, questioning expression.*
4. *Her hair is a beautiful light brown though not noticeably abundant.*	*Her hair is remarkably fair, almost silver-gilt, and exceptionally thick and wavy.*
5. *The loose-fitting morning costume she is wearing is in good style.* (272)	*She is wearing a dark calling costume, of a good style but not of the latest fashion.* (278)

This close and deliberate parallelism between the two passages of directions invites a comparative consideration of the characters and their relationship from the outset. Hedda's dominance is indexed here at the levels of age, class position, temperament and dress, and the contrast is reinforced by the use of terminology connoting the childlike to describe Mrs Elvsted. In the context of performance, Mrs Elvsted is identified by Hedda, in the course of a conversation with Tesman, immediately prior to her entrance. The greater part of the scene that ensues is given over to a duologue between the two women (282–9), which establishes both the terms of their relationship and the function of foil to Hedda for the character of Mrs Elvsted. With regard to stage action, Hedda's assertion of control is expressed graphically by the adoption of dominant positions (e.g. *'leaning against the arm of the chair'* in which Mrs Elvsted is seated: 285), and by the recurrent use of physical force to intimidate the latter, who is described as a *'slender little thing'*:

> *She pulls* MRS ELVSTED *down on to the sofa* . . . (279).
> *She pushes* MRS ELVSTED *into the easy-chair by the stove* . . . (282).
> *giving her a little slap on the hand* (284).

pinching her arm (323).
She pulls MRS ELVSTED, *almost by force, towards the doorway* (325).

Mrs Elvsted, characterised by a *'startled, questioning expression'*, responds with a consistent level of anxiety to the sustained physical and verbal onslaught to which she is subjected: *'gives her a frightened glance . . .'* (280); *'starting nervously'*; *'getting up quickly, in some distress'* (281); *'alarmed'* (282); *'looking anxiously at her watch'* (283); *'gazing helplessly in front of her'* (284); *'looking at her doubtfully'* (285); *'with a faint cry'*; *'in suppressed anxiety'* (323).

We shall pursue this contrast further in relation to one specific detail, the representation in the establishing stage directions of the hair of the two characters. Difference is articulated in terms both of colour (*'a beautiful light brown'/'remarkably fair, almost silver-gilt'*) and of quality (*'not noticeably abundant'/ 'exceptionally thick and wavy'*). The brunette/blonde opposition has particular cultural connotations, and intersects with a set of congruent polarities: adult/childlike; worldly/unworldly; active/passive; hard/soft. It is possible, moreover, in the light of the subsequent action, to infer a metaphorical significance for the respective heads of hair: to read Mrs Elvsted's as an index of creativity and fertility, Hedda's in contrast, as indexing the lack of these capacities. Repeated reference is made to Mrs Elvsted's hair in both the directions and the dialogue. We will now consider the theatrical and thematic implications of these references.

Hedda's initial identification of Mrs Elvsted indicates a negative relation to the latter's hair and, by extension, to Mrs Elvsted herself: 'That girl with the tiresome hair, that she was always showing off' (278). Almost as soon as the two women are left alone by Tesman, Mrs Elvsted raises the issue in the context of shared schooldays, articulating a remembered fear of Hedda:

MRS E. . . . How dreadfully frightened of you I was in those days!

HEDDA. Were you frightened of me?

MRS E. Yes. Dreadfully frightened. Because when we met on the stairs you always used to pull my hair.

127

HEDDA. No, *did* I?

MRS E. Yes, and once you said you would burn it off.

(283)

The schooldays scenario is evoked at the close of Act II, as an expression of Hedda's envy of Mrs Elvsted's 'reclamation' of and friendship with Ejlert Lovberg:

HEDDA. . . . (*Throwing her arms passionately round her.*) I think I shall burn your hair off, after all.

MRS E. Let go! Let go! I'm frightened of you, Hedda!

(324)

When, at the close of Act III, Hedda burns the manuscript that is the product of the Mrs Elvsted–Lovberg friendship, she personifies it as the child of that friendship and couples its destruction to a further reference to Mrs Elvsted's hair:

HEDDA (*throwing some of the leaves into the fire and whispering to herself*). Now I am burning your child, Thea. You, with your curly hair. (*Throwing a few more leaves into the stove.*) Your child and Ejlert Lovberg's. (*Throwing in the rest.*) I'm burning it – burning your child.

(345)

Three additional directions indicate that Hedda is to touch Mrs Elvsted's hair in the course of the action. In Act II, working to disrupt the Mrs Elvsted–Lovberg friendship, she insists that Mrs Elvsted sit beside her on the sofa rather than in a chair adjacent to Lovberg's: 'I want to be in the middle.' In proxemic terms, the arrangement of the actors' bodies in stage space constitutes an externalisation of the psychodynamic of the scene. Hedda's dominance is apparent, further, in the infantilisation of Mrs Elvsted, whom she addresses as 'Thea my child', and whom she proceeds to pet, '*stroking her hair lightly*' (319). There are two variations on the gesture towards the close of the play, between the report of Lovberg's death by misadventure and the suicide of Hedda. In the first instance, Hedda stands '*behind* MRS ELVSTED*'s chair, ruffling her hair gently*', as the latter and Tesman embark upon the task of reconstituting from Lovberg's notes the destroyed manuscript (360). There

128

follows a brief scene with Brack, whose attempt to blackmail Hedda sexually determines her course of suicide. She takes a veiled farewell of Mrs Elvsted, a final human contact which suggests both a reconciliation and the bequeathing of Tesman:

HEDDA. . . . . (*Letting her hands stray gently through* MRS ELVSTED's hair.) Doesn't it feel strange to you, Thea? Here you are sitting with Jorgen Tesman just as you once sat with Ejlert Lovberg.

MRS E. Well, if only I could inspire your husband too –

HEDDA. Oh, that will come all right – in time

(362)

With regard to the actor, the classification of intra- and extra-dialogic directions given in Chapter 5 is organised in terms of a series of descriptive functions. We may proceed from here to an examination of a broader set of theatrical and thematic functions inscribed in the extra-dialogic directions. In both cases it will be apparent that the actor has much to gain from giving due attention to stage directions.

The preceding discussion of *Hedda Gabler* focused upon the appearance and characterisation of two characters, Hedda and Mrs Elvsted, in relation to one another. The interaction of characters, both physical and psychological, is of crucial interest to the actor. The proxemic relations indicated in the directions serve to reflect issues of status and control. External/physical modes of relating serve to index internal/psychological conditions and conflicts. Information may be offered on the identity and subjectivity of a character, and on the character's significance to the action, the thematic concerns and/or the ideological underpinnings of the text.

The directions may carry references to, or have implications for, performance style and pitch of action. In *Lady Audley's Secret*, for example, the directions for the attempted murder of George Talboys by Lady Audley are couched in terms that define a melodramatic acting style:

LADY AUDLEY (*striking him with the iron handle*). It is indeed – die!
(*Pushes him down the well, the ruined stones fall with him.*)
He is gone – gone! and no one was a witness to the deed!

129

. . . *(Raises her arms in triumph, laughing exultingly . . .)*
(248)

In *The Cherry Orchard*, conversely, the directions work in conjunction with the dialogue to build an effect of naturalism, to reproduce by means of an aesthetic of verisimilitude the surface impression of everyday life.

The directions may convey also a sense of the stage–spectator relationship. The 'bourgeois' text maintains a focus within the illusionistic frame via the operation of the 'fourth wall' convention. The 'radical' text is likely to break the frame, in order to shift the terms of interaction with the spectator. Hence, in *The Mother*, Vlasova addresses the audience directly, offering a commentary on her manipulation of the porter at the factory gates (154). At the close of the play, she *'recites'* to the spectators an exhortation to accept and act upon the political analysis furnished by the text.

It is possible to argue, further, that stage directions may exercise thematic or ideological functions, and that the attention given to them may serve also to enhance the actor's understanding of the thematic concerns or social resonance of the specific text. In *The Cherry Orchard*, for example, affectations of gentility on the part of the servants Dooniasha and Yasha, as they ape the manners of their class 'superiors', point to the breaking down of the old order and a blurring of social distinctions.

DOONIASHA *(agitated)*. I'm going to faint . . . Oh I'm fainting! . . . (335)

YASHA *(crossing the stage, in an affectedly genteel voice)*. May I go through here? (339).

In *The Mother*, the directions concerning the operation of the duplicating machine in scene 2 and the printing press in scene 9 communicate a sense of the danger entailed in the writing and reproduction of revolutionary propaganda.

Additional information on these various points may of course be extrapolated from the dialogue. The dialogue itself, moreover, may reflexively carry information on how the actor is formally to speak it, in terms of punctuation and phrasing, for instance. The most recurrent direction in *Endgame* is *'pause'* (French *un temps*, a space of time). The insistent punctuation of the text, both literally and in performance, with the direction draws attention to the shaping theme, defined by Richard Coe as 'the *angoisse* of man at grips with time, the finite clutching at the infinite' (1964: 92), and to the self-referentiality of the work:

HAMM: . . . Silence! (*Pause.*) Where was I? (*Pause. Gloomily.*) It's finished, we're finished. (*Pause.*) Nearly finished. (*Pause.*) There'll be no more speech. (*Pause.*)

(35)

STAGE DIRECTIONS AND DIALOGUE

In general, the extra-dialogic directions which frame the dramatic dialogue serve variously to explicate and/or otherwise reinforce and/or position the reader in relation to that dialogue. On occasion, however, in the service of a specific effect of disjunction, directions and dialogue may be so articulated as to be in conflict. The interaction of stage direction with stage direction is informed, in comparable manner, by the possibilities of complementarity and contradiction. The general expectation is that systems of staging will be operated interdependently, and in parallel. Again, this expectation may on occasion be subverted.

It follows that we can define four modes of relationship, structured in terms of either complementarity or contradiction, respectively between stage directions and dialogue, and between direction and direction.

1. Stage directions and dialogue as mutually supportive. In *Top Girls*, the adolescent Angie fantasises the murder of her supposed mother, her aunt Joyce:

ANGIE. I'm going to kill my mother and you're going to watch.

KIT. I'm not playing.

ANGIE. You're scared of blood.

KIT *puts her hand under her dress, brings it out with blood on her finger.*

KIT. There, see, I got my own blood, so.

ANGIE *takes* KIT's *hand and licks her finger.*

131

ANGIE. Now I'm a cannibal. I might turn into a vampire now.
(35–6)

2. Stage directions and dialogue in conflict. At the close of
Endgame, Clov's unsuccessful attempt to leave the stage, and
Hamm, is constructed in ironic and self-referential terms:

CLOV: . . . I open the door of the cell and go . . . (*Pause.*) It's
easy going. (*Pause.*) When I fall I'll weep for happiness.
Pause. He goes towards the door.

HAMM. Clov! (CLOV *halts, without turning.*) Nothing. (CLOV *moves
on.*) Clov!
CLOV *halts without turning.*

CLOV. This is what we call making an exit.

(51)

3. Systems of staging as mutually supportive. Act III of *The
Cherry Orchard* opens with a ball, or, in the rather more precise
phrase used by Liubov Andryeevna in anticipation of the event,
'a little dance' (360). The directions for setting, lighting, action,
dialogue and costume work in concert to convey a sense of the
environment, the dancing and the atmosphere:

> *The drawing-room of the Ranyevskaias' house. Adjoining the
> drawing-room at the back, and connected to it by an archway
> is the ballroom. A Jewish band . . . is heard playing in the hall.
> It is evening; the candles in a chandelier are alight. In the ball-
> room a party is dancing the Grand-Rond.* SIMEONOV-PISHCHIK
> *is heard to call out: 'Promenade à une paire!', then all come
> into the drawing room . . .* FEERS, *wearing a tail-coat, crosses
> the room with soda-water on a tray.*

(370)

4. Systems of staging in conflict. The establishing directions
in *Hedda Gabler* offer detailed and precise notes for the play's
setting. The basic stage picture is constructed from contrasting
elements. The drawing-room is crowded with furniture and
'*decorated in dark colours*'. The resulting sense of oppressiveness
is offset by sunlight, which '*shines in through the glass doors*', and
by the profusion of bouquets of flowers (263).

The stage picture, and its levels of operation, will receive
detailed consideration in Chapter 8.

DESIGN AND TECHNICAL ELEMENTS

As in the case of the actor, the directions which are relevant to the work of the designer, the lighting designer and the technician may be regarded as constituting an outline brief.

With regard to the designer, the present discussion will focus on costume; setting will be considered in some detail in Chapter 8. Again, it will be helpful to use the three-phase developmental model.

1. The 'classic' text

In the absence for the most part of explicit extra-dialogic directions in 'classic' texts, it is in general a feasible proposition for the designer to extrapolate a basic commission from the dialogue and from historical source materials. (We have provided an example of this process in Chapter 5.) Hence the designer has the option of using hieratic costumes and masks for Greek plays, emblematic costumes for the personified abstractions of medieval drama, and elaborations of the social costume of the day for Elizabethan and Jacobean work.

We may take as a single instance the actor's mask for the title role in *Oedipus the King*. Oedipus is characterised at the opening of the play as a mature, dignified and responsible ruler. The design of the mask, for a production opting to use masks, would need to reflect this character. In terms of aesthetic considerations, the designer might well have recourse, for example, to vase-paintings contemporaneous with the play. Taplin argues for a change of mask for the character's final entrance, on the grounds of Sophocles' 'exploitation of the downright physical shock of Oedipus' bloody empty eyes'. On this view, the actor is assumed to have changed the first mask for 'one with dark eye-sockets with streams of blood running down from them' (Taplin 1985: 89).

2. The 'bourgeois' text

It is possible to trace an increasing emphasis on detail and explicitness in stage directions concerned with design issues, as the modern period develops.

133

Lady Audley's Secret (1985 [1862]) assumes costumes reflective of class positions, and provides detail in respect of significant variations only. Hence Luke Marks, *'a drunken gamekeeper'*, is *'dressed in velveteen coat, flowered waistcoat, and cord breeches and gaiters, and has a rough dissipated appearance'* (236–7). The other variations from conventional attire are occasion-specific: Alicia is at one point dressed *'in a riding habit'* (240); Robert Audley *'in mourning'* (252).

The directions in *Hedda Gabler* (1950 [1890]) provide a detailed indication of character-specific costume at the first entrance of each character.

MISS TESMAN: '. . . *wearing her hat and carrying a parasol . . . well but simply dressed in grey outdoor clothes'.* (263)

TESMAN: '. . . *he wears glasses. He is comfortably – almost carelessly – dressed, in an outdoor suit.'* (266)

HEDDA: *'The loose-fitting morning costume she is wearing is in good style.'* (272)

MRS ELVSTED: *'She is wearing a dark calling costume, of a good style but not quite of the latest fashion.'* (278)

JUDGE BRACK: *'He is dressed in a well-cut outdoor suit – a little too young for his age. He wears an eye-glass.'* (289)

EJLERT LOVBERG: *'He is dressed in a well-cut black suit, quite new, and is carrying dark gloves and a top-hat.'* (308)

Costume is employed here to index the dramatis personae in terms of character, self-image and self-presentation, and social and economic status. It may be used to denote similarity or difference, as we have observed with regard to Hedda and Mrs Elvsted, and to reflect the social conventions of the period and milieu. Hence distinctions are apparent between 'outdoor' and 'indoor' and between formal and informal clothing.

The well-to-do changed outfits according both to time of day and to occasion. Hedda wears *'morning costume'* in Act I and *'an afternoon dress'* in Act II (296). Mrs Elvsted returns in Act II *'dressed for the evening'* (318), whereas in Act I she wears a *'calling costume'*. Brack in Act II is *'dressed as for an informal party'* (296), and Tesman changes here from *'a grey outdoor suit and a soft felt hat'* (301) to appropriate dress for the same party

(307). In Act IV, consequent upon the death of Lovberg, Hedda is 'dressed in black', Berte the maid wears 'black ribbons in her cap', and Miss Tesman is 'dressed in mourning, with a hat and veil' (346).

3. The 'radical' text

While the issue of costume is not explicitly addressed by the directions in either *The Mother* or *Top Girls*, a strategy is apparent in both plays. The characters in *The Mother* are defined in social rather than psychological terms, and costume should therefore reflect class position and occupation. In *Top Girls*, the costumes worn by the guests at Marlene's dinner-party are determined by their respective historical, artistic or literary points of origin. The characters drawn from Marlene's public life in the present, i.e. the employment agency, or those grouped in the flashbacks to her past private life, i.e. the scenes with Joyce, Kit and Angie, are, like Brecht's characters in *The Mother*, defined in social terms, and so are to be dressed with a view to reinforcing class and gender issues.

In *Endgame* the directions construct an approach to make-up and costume which positions the spectator to confront the characters as metaphorical representations. Clov and Hamm are described as having 'very red' faces (11, 12), Nagg and Nell as having 'very white' (15, 18). No information is offered on Clov's costume until the close of the play, where an inventory is given of his outfit for the journey he is unable to make: *'Enter* CLOV, *dressed for the road. Panama hat, tweed coat, raincoat over his arm, umbrella, bag'* (51). Hamm, in contrast, is described in detail at the outset: *'Centre, in an armchair on castors, covered with an old sheet,* HAMM ... *In a dressing gown, a stiff toque on his head, a large blood-stained handkerchief over his face, a whistle hanging from his neck, a rug over his knees, thick socks on his feet'* (11–12). Nagg and Nell, heads occasionally protruding from their 'ashbins', are attired respectively in a 'nightcap' (15) and a 'lace cap' (18).

The final section of Table 5.1. is concerned with directions for lighting and sound effects. These, and such specialised technical effects as the proliferation of matter in Ionesco's work (e.g. *Amedée or How to Get Rid of It, The Future is in Eggs*) and the disintegration and ultimate disappearance of the set in the same author's *Exit the King*, constitute issues for discussion between the director and/or designer and the appropriate technical personnel.

SYNTHESIS: SYSTEMS OF STAGING

The theatrical project of extra-dialogic stage directions is fore-grounded in Pirandello's *Six Characters in Search of an Author* in several extended passages of 'author's notes', to resort without prejudice to Veltruský's terms (1977: 48–9). Pirandello, regarding an absolute differentiation between 'Characters' and 'Actors' as essential to the spectator's effective reception of the play in performance, here proposes a synthesis of systems of staging as the logical means of determining the requisite degree of difference. An examination of his proposal serves both to consolidate the discussion thus far and to offer a salutary reminder that systems of staging, while often necessarily considered in isolation, are mutually interdependent. It may be noted, also, that the orchestration of these systems – the processes of selection and combination, relations of complementarity and contradiction, and relative emphases at specific points in a production – constitutes a key aspect of the work of the director.

In *Six Characters*, the two groups are differentiated unequivocally with regard to appearance, performance style, position within stage space, and lighting. Pirandello's detailed notes on the Characters, placed after the directions for their first entrance, begin as follows:

> In any production of this play it is imperative that the producer should use every means possible to avoid any confusion between the SIX CHARACTERS and the ACTORS. The placings of the two groups, as they will be indicated in the stage-directions once the CHARACTERS are on the stage, will no doubt help. So, too, will their being lit in different colours. But the most effective and most suitable method of distinguishing them that suggests itself, is the use of special masks for the CHARACTERS . . .

The characters are envisaged as 'unchangeable creations of the imagination' and hence as 'more real and more consistent than the ever-changing naturalness' of the Actors (6). The Actors, a company of 'nine or ten', are therefore given an establishing

136

'*improvised scene*' which is to be played '*very naturally and with great vivacity*'. It is, however, an improvisation which is tightly structured by the text, a perhaps inevitable consequence of the time of writing (1921):

> *While they are waiting – some of them standing, some seated about in small groups – they exchange a few words among themselves. One lights a cigarette, another complains about the part that he's been given and a third reads out an item of news from a theatrical journal for the benefit of the other actors. . . . After a while, one of the comedy men can sit down at the piano and start playing a dance-tune. The younger* ACTORS *and* ACTRESSES *start dancing.*

(2)

The Characters, in contrast, enact the scenes of their uncompleted play in a 'theatrical' and insistently self-referential manner:

PRODUCER. And where's the script?

FATHER. It is in us, sir. (*The* ACTORS *laugh.*) The drama is in us. *We* are the drama and we are impatient to act it – so fiercely does our inner passion urge us on.

STEPDAUGHTER (*scornful, treacherous, alluring, with deliberate shamelessness*). My passion. . . . If only you knew! My passion . . . for him!
(*She points to the* FATHER *and makes as if to embrace him, but then bursts into strident laughter.*

(11)

Whereas the faces of the Actors, as they wait to begin their rehearsal (of another Pirandello play, *The Game As He Played It*), may be supposed to be made up 'naturally', the masks of the Characters are intended to '*assist in giving the impression of figures constructed by art, each one fixed immutably in the expression of that sentiment which is fundamental to it*'. It follows that the Characters are conceived as personified abstractions, each animated by a single, shaping passion: '*remorse for the* FATHER, *revenge for the* STEPDAUGHTER, *contempt for the* SON *and sorrow for the* MOTHER'. (The two Characters not mentioned here are the Mother's younger children, the innocent victims of the family drama.) The Mother's mask, to take a single example,

137

'should have wax tears fixed in the corners of the eyes and coursing down the cheeks, just like those which are carved and painted in the representations of the Mater Dolorosa that are to be seen in churches'.

The analogy with fine art is extended from mask to costume. It is stipulated that the Mother's dress *'should be of a special material and cut. It should be severely plain, its folds stiff, giving in fact the appearance of having been carved . . .'* (6). The dress is *'a modest black'*, and the Mother also wears *'a thick crêpe widow's veil'*. The Stepdaughter, too, *'is dressed in mourning'* and the Father wears *'a dark jacket'* (7). The costumes of the Characters are in strong contrast to those of the Actors: *'It would be best if all the ACTORS and ACTRESSES could be dressed in rather bright and gay clothes'* (2). The Leading Lady, who is to take the role of the Stepdaughter when the Actors attempt to rehearse the Characters' scenes, is encoded in diametric opposition to the female Characters, in terms of colour, style and impact: *'She is dressed completely in white, with a large and rather dashing and provocative hat, and is carrying a dainty little lap-dog'* (3).

Finally, there are directions for the respective positions of the two groups on stage, and for the deployment of lighting as a further means of marking off the constructed from the 'natural', the role from the 'real'. The Characters make their initial entrance from the auditorium. After an opening exchange with the producer, the Father *'holds out his hand to the MOTHER and . . . leads her with a certain tragic solemnity to the other side of the stage'* from that occupied by the Actors. As they move into position, the area *'immediately lights up with a fantastic kind of light'* (9–10). At the climax of the play, *'a green flood'* is used to project *'the silhouettes of the CHARACTERS . . . , clear-cut and huge, on to the backcloth'* (69).

The differentiation between Characters and Actors, then, is fundamental to Pirandello's overarching objective, a theatricalised and self-referential debate on the subject of theatrical representation. To this end, regular and detailed use is made of extra-dialogic directions which frequently shade into 'author's notes'. At this point, we may return briefly to the issue of authorial control as noted earlier in relation to the arguments of Elam and Pavis. It is, of course, possible to argue that Pirandello is seeking to determine the direction of any subsequent production of the text via the provision of close guidelines. A more open-minded and constructive reading might be that the dramatist is conscious of posing a series of quite considerable problems, both aesthetic and conceptual, for the reader/spectator, and that he has in consequence recorded his own solutions. These may be regarded as suggestions, rather than as prescriptive. The individual director has the options of acceptance or negotiation or rejection of the stage directions, once full and systematic cognisance has been taken of them in the course of the rehearsal process.

Six Characters in Search of an Author is a 'radical' text in that it draws attention to its textuality by means of a consistent focus on the mechanisms of dramatic and theatrical signification. Hence, as was noted in respect of the 'radical' text in Chapter 5, the stage directions work to inscribe a mode of theatricality that foregrounds its status *as* theatricality. This anti-illusionistic aesthetic is taken a stage further in *Endgame*, a metatheatrical text which is not set in a theatrical milieu.

The Hamm–Clov interaction operates on a number of interdependent levels. On the level of metatheatricality, both characters are represented as actors, each with his own 'speciality' (16); Hamm fancies himself as a narrator, Clov begins the play as a mime. Moreover, Hamm is identified variously with the functions of playwright and director, Clov with those of a stage-manager. The opening block of stage directions serves both to outline the initial stage picture and to prescribe, in precise detail, Clov's establishing sequence of mime. A *'brief tableau'* is broken by Clov's *'stiff, staggering walk'*. Attention is thus focused on the process of performance from the outset. Clov prepares, and so defines, the playing space in a sequence of patterned moves: climbing, by means of a ladder, to two high windows upstage left and right, to draw back curtains; removing the sheet covering the two ashbins downstage right and checking their contents; removing the sheet covering Hamm and looking him over. Having discharged this responsibility of on-stage stage-manager, as the play plays with and blurs the distinction between the conventions of rehearsal and performance, Clov *'turns towards* [the] *auditorium'*, breaking the illusionistic frame with the play's opening speech.

Clov's mime serves also to establish the terms of the performance, and hence the terms of the stage–spectator relationship, as a brief extract from the directions will demonstrate:

139

He gets down, goes with ladder towards ashbins, halts, turns,
carries back ladder and sets it down under window right, goes
to ashbins, removes sheet covering them, folds it over his arm.
He raises one lid, stoops and looks into bin. Brief laugh. He
closes lid. Same with other bin.

(11–12)

The mime is characterised by an uncertain purposefulness,
as Clov continually checks and readjusts the sequence of his
movements, and by a pattern of repetition that is often symmet-
rical. The modernist text, in performance, invites consideration
of its formal operations, offers its form as a mode of content.
The spectator, confronted with a metaphorical dimension at
the levels of both setting and action, is confronted also with
the necessity of adjusting her/his habits of spectatorship.

As we noted in the prefatory remarks to Chapter 5, stage
directions have tended to receive an unprofitably scant level
of attention in critical and theoretical discussion. In our view,
the study of the dramatic text (whether for academic or professional purposes) may be considerably enhanced by the application of two straightforward exercises.

1. If, when one first approaches a text, the stage directions
are marked by highlighting or underlining, one is thereafter
almost compelled to engage with them, and so to develop a
sense of how the dramatist has envisaged the stage pictures
and 'heard' the dialogue.

2. If one translates stage directions for settings, and for
groupings and key movements, into outline sketches or diagrams, one develops a clear sense of the nature and significance
of the characters' environment, and of proxemic and kinesic
'sign-posting'.

Chapter 8, an extended examination of the visual dimension of theatre, begins with a consideration of the processes
whereby the spectator is 'confronted' with a *mise-en-scène* that
is constituted by the director and her/his collaborators, in
response to the dramatist's encoding, in the form of stage
directions, of setting and stage picture.

8

READING THE IMAGE

As in the case of stage directions, the visual dimension of theatre is in general accorded a somewhat surprisingly low priority in critical and theoretical discussion. Reviewers on occasion pay some regard to the work of the set or costume designer. Collections of designs are published, usually in the manner of 'coffee table' books. Like catalogues for design exhibitions, they tend to be confined to a selection of illustrations, and biographical material on the participating designers. The catalogue for the recent exhibition 'British Theatre Design: 1983–1987' (Ackermann et al. 1987) constitutes a representative example. The exhibition was assembled as a showcase for the work of members of the Society of British Theatre Designers. A significant proportion of the designs exhibited were complex and challenging, but no attempt was made, either in the exhibition itself or in the catalogue, to provide a contextual and critical framework. One commendable exception to this regrettable rule is John Willett's analytical monograph on Caspar Neher, who designed for Brecht throughout the latter's working life, published to accompany a touring exhibition of Neher's work selected by Willett and organised by the Arts Council of Great Britain (1986).

In Chapters 5 and 7 we examined stage directions in relation to the systems of staging which intersect in the construction of stage pictures – setting, costume, properties and lighting – and in relation to the facial and physical work of the actor, the dynamic element in the (generally) static theatrical frame. In Chapter 6 we considered the actor as sign. We are concerned in the present chapter to develop an analysis of the ways in which these various theatrical sign-systems are deployed to construct stage pictures, i.e. how the written text comes to signify production and performance style.

We shall begin by separating out the phases and processes of encoding and decoding involved, from the dramatist's envisioning of the stage space to the spectator's engagement with that space as realised by the director and designer. We shall then discuss the levels of operation of the stage picture and the serial development of discrete images into visual metaphor. Finally, through reference to social semiotics and to painting as an analogous form, we shall address the role of the spectator.

ENCODINGS/DECODINGS

The spectator's reception of the visual dimension is to be seen as the final stage of a project that involves four distinct phases:

1 The dramatist encodes the text in terms of her/his perception of its function as a blueprint for theatrical production.
2 The director decodes the text, initiates a process of commission or collaboration with a production team and arrives at a *mise-en-scène*.
3 The designer re-encodes the text to develop a portfolio of designs, within a pre-determined or negotiated brief and subject to interpretative, spatial and budgetary constraints.
4 The spectator decodes the production, works upon and is worked upon by the visual dimension as an integral aspect of the reception process.

It goes almost without saying that, from the earliest theatres, dramatists have been concerned to counterpoint verbal with visual impact. We have only to cite the chorus of Furies in the *Eumenides* of Aeschylus or the animal choruses of Aristophanes, the mansions representing Heaven and Hell in medieval scenic disposition, and the dumb shows of Elizabethan and Jacobean tragedy. With the development of the profession of the designer in the modern period, the writer of a 'bourgeois' or 'radical' dramatic text has the option of pre-designing, as it were, an environment and a style of costuming appropriate to narrative and character, and to the thematic concerns and theatrical pitch of the play. Letters from Chekhov, to Nemirovich-Danchenko and to Stanislavsky respectively, indicate his thinking with regard

142

to the second and third acts of *The Cherry Orchard*. 'In Act Two of my play I've substituted an old chapel and a well for the river. It's more peaceful that way. Only in Act Two you must give me some proper green fields and a road and a sense of distance unusual on the stage' (Lyman 1976: 173–4). 'The house in the play has two stories [*sic*] and is large. After all there is a mention in Act Three of a staircase going downstairs' (ibid.: 177). Ibsen's notes for *Hedda Gabler* offer a beguiling image that did not survive in the finished version of the text. 'The newly wedded couple return home in September – as the summer is dying. In the second act they sit in the garden – but with their coats on' (Cole 1960: 160). It does not of course follow that all dramatists are equally interested in, or regard themselves as competent to provide more than outline suggestions in respect of the visual dimension of production. The directions for setting in *The Mother* and *Top Girls*, for example, are spare. Brecht, as has been noted, worked in an ongoing collaboration with Neher, who designed the 1932 Berlin production. Hence, the provision of additional scenographic detail would have been superfluous to need. Churchill may well have preferred to leave issues of design to Max Stafford-Clark and Peter Hartwell, the director and designer of the 1982 Royal Court production. However, her conjoining of characters drawn from Brueghel, Chaucer, and western and eastern history suggests an active visual imagination. Beckett's establishing directions for *Endgame*, laconic but precise, project a strong metaphorical resonance:

Bare interior.
Grey light.
Left and right back, high up, two small windows, curtains drawn. Front right, a door. Hanging near door, its face to wall, a picture. Front left, touching each other, covered with an old sheet, two ashbins. Centre, in an armchair on castors, covered with an old sheet, HAMM. *Motionless by the door, his eyes fixed on* HAMM, CLOV. *Very red face. Brief tableau.*

(11)

We shall return to questions of visual metaphor in due course.

When the director approaches a text with production in mind, she/he has three options in relation to the dramatist's directions: acceptance, or adaptation, or rejection. One might argue that it is a matter of simple common sense to explore, and attempt to come to terms with, the dramatist's suggestions for the environment inhabited by the characters, to take the immediate example. Yet such does not appear invariably to be the case. It is less than difficult to think of productions where the pictorial sub-text has been distorted or wholly lost as a consequence of directorial intervention. We do not have the space here to propose an ethics of directing, but it may be argued that the function involves a threefold responsibility: towards the text, towards the director's co-workers, and towards the spectator. The spectator has the right to expect a realisation of the text which is as complete, appropriate and focused as the director and her/his collaborators are able to contrive.

The designer's capacity to contribute to the process of realisation is dependent upon the director's willingness to consult. The designer may be offered a commission which covers all the pictorial components, costumes and properties as well as setting, and thus the opportunity to develop an overall design concept for the production. The design contribution may be limited to the functionalistic or merely decorative. Conversely, it may be integral to the realisation of the text, counterpointing theme and ideology, image and symbol, in pictorial terms. The point is made effectively in an account of Bob Crowley's designs for the 1989 National Theatre production of *Hedda Gabler*:

> A miraculous circle with a black stove as its centrepiece; a chimney flue forms its axis – and lets out real smoke. Crowley's set is more than a background for Hedda – it encloses her. . . . The trees are dead, the books wait behind wire, the yellow leaves that Hedda notices are pasted against the glass. The atmosphere suggests that nothing can come to any good. The strange verdigris-coloured sofa is adorned with golden griffins as fierce as Hedda herself. Crowley has a touch of the poet when it comes to costume, too: Hedda moves from wedded white to an incendiary's red, to mourning black in the third [*sic*] act.
>
> (Kellaway 1989)

These designs self-evidently derive from a process of consultation between Crowley and Howard Davies, the director.

A debate held at the Riverside Studios in May 1987 addressed the question, 'Directors and Designers – What Kind of a Collaboration?' A set of related points were raised recurrently in the course of the debate. The training of the designer rarely pays account to textual analysis. The training of the director, in so far as such training exists, rarely conduces to a visual 'literacy'. These points find reinforcement in the recent Gulbenkian Foundation enquiry into the training of the director:

> Discussions with a number of designers revealed that . . . there is no protocol to guide the director and the designer. How a director briefs a designer and how they work together after that varies from individual to individual.
>
> It appears that a large number of directors do not adequately appreciate the full potential of a designer's contribution to the production. Consequently the relationship has often been fraught with misunderstandings, conflicts and lack of communication . . .
>
> (Rea 1989: 64–5)

A *lingua franca*, a shared language, needs to be developed in order to facilitate both an informed and informing process of collaboration and, in consequence, a more theorised and ambitious practice of design.

Where a visual 'literacy' on the part of the designer operates in conjunction with a successful director–designer collaboration (and despite our general, pessimistic overview, exceptions such as Brecht/Neher and Brook/Jacobs do exist), it follows that the encoding of the visual dimension of the production will benefit (as will the spectator's pleasure in the decoding/reception process). A more recent example of what appears to be a successful working collaboration between director and designer, witnessed in the visual dimension of a stage production, is Richard Hudson's setting for Jonathan Miller's realisation of *Andromaque*, performed at the Old Vic in 1988. (The tragedies of Racine are currently enjoying something of a revival in Britain. *Britannicus* was staged at the Crucible Theatre, Sheffield, *Berenice* at the National Theatre and *Bajazet* at the Almeida Theatre, all in 1990.) Hudson's setting for *Andromaque* established a surrealistic classicism – opaque windows, stairways to nowhere, an impractically steep rake – as the appropriate visual style for the prison-house world of these plays. In her essay, 'The Space of *Phèdre*', Anne Ubersfeld argues that Troezen, 'the *here* of the tragedy, is a prison one vainly dreams of escaping. . . . For Phèdre Troezen is "walls" and "vaults". For Hippolyte it is the prison of sex, and all attempts to break out of it are doomed' (1981: 205). On this view, Hudson's setting may be read, both literally and symbolically, as constituting a denial of flight. Furthermore, Hudson's visual contribution counters difficulties which inevitably arise in the process of crossing historical, cultural, theatrical and linguistic boundaries in the course of translating theatre texts/performance contexts. Where the sense of 'no escape' is signified in the source text by means of the linguistic sign-system – the regular, closed world of the classical alexandrine verse structure – a translation equivalent in the British production is found in the designer's pictorial system of signification. This reinforces our suggestion that the work in phases two and three of theatrical production requires close collaboration, in order to maximise the spectator's engagement in the final, fourth phase.

We shall consider the spectator's engagement with the design elements of production in due course.

STAGE PICTURE: LEVELS OF OPERATION

In this section we shall argue that the stage picture operates on four distinct, if potentially interdependent, levels, that discrete elements in a single picture may operate differentially, and that an individual element may be invested with a range of character-specific values.

The levels of operation are as follows:

1 Functionalistic. The dialogue of *As You Like It*, III.2, commissions a tree to which Orlando may affix his love-lyric in praise of Rosalind (61). The stage directions of *Lady Audley's Secret* indicate that a practical flight of steps to the hayloft is required for II.3 (260). In such cases, the primary demand made upon the designer is a practical one. That said, the tree may well contribute to the production in terms of atmosphere, the flight of steps in symbolic terms.

2 Sociometric. Reference has already been made to the use of the mask in Greek theatre as an index of rank and gender

146

(see Chapter 5). The establishing directions of *Hedda Gabler* describe *'a large drawing-room, well furnished, in good taste'* (263), a reflection of the comfortable middle-class life-style of the original audience. Scene 8.b of *The Mother* is set in an estate kitchen. Strike-breakers converse while the estate butcher chops meat (182). While the conventions of representation obtaining for 'classic', 'bourgeois' and 'radical' texts are markedly divergent, each example suggests a concern to define social status in pictorial terms. Taken together, the examples offer a particular version of the history of the subject in drama: a downwardly socially mobile trajectory, from the nobility of the 'classic' text, via the gentry/mercantile middle class of the 'bourgeois' text, to the 'people' of the 'radical' text.

3 Atmospheric. The city of Thebes, in *Oedipus the King*, is afflicted with plague. The expositional tableau vivant, and the choreographic dimension of the entry-song of the chorus, respectively reinforce spoken dialogue and sung lyric at the level of the stage picture. The dialogue of *As You Like It* inscribes a structural contrast between oppressive court and liberating forest. One cannot envisage a modern production failing to underline this contrast pictorially. The *Hedda Gabler* drawing-room is *'decorated in dark colours'*. Taken in conjunction with the inventory of numerous items of furniture, and the taste of the bourgeoisie of the period for solid and substantial furniture design and for the conspicuous display of possessions as indicative of social standing, the prescription of a sombre palette for the designer suggests a stage environment that is both enervating and claustrophobic. It might then be argued that Ibsen was concerned to replicate, in the spectator's experience of the stage picture, the social experience of the play's protagonist.

4 Symbolic. In medieval drama, both scenic disposition and character representation are encoded in highly symbolic ways. In *Everyman*, God is enthroned apart 'in the high seat celestial' (211), and the personified abstractions Goods and Good Deeds are respectively immobilised by cupidity and by the lack of righteous action on the part of Everyman:

> I lie here in corners, trussed and piled so high,
> And in chests I am locked so fast,

Also sacked in bags. Thou mayst see with thine eye
I cannot stir; in packs low I lie.   (218)

Here I lie, cold in the ground;
Thy sins hath me sore bound,
That I cannot stir.   (221)

In *Endgame*, Hamm has confined the living, human refuse
of his parents to the pair of ashbins prominently set front
left.

A brief survey of Arthur Miller's directions for the setting
of *Death of a Salesman* will demonstrate the interaction of the
four levels of operation of the stage picture. The focal point
is the house of the Loman family. Three rooms are visible,
the kitchen, the parents' bedroom and the boys' bedroom,
as is the back yard. The house is furnished sparsely, and in
terms of the demands of the action. It stands as an index
of a working-class family beset by hard times. Of particular
interest is the relation of the house to other elements of the
stage picture.

> *Before us is the* SALESMAN'S *house. We are aware of towering,
> angular shapes behind it, surrounding it on all sides. Only the
> blue light of the sky falls upon the house and forestage; the
> surrounding area shows an angry glow of orange. As more
> light appears, we see a solid vault of apartment houses around
> the small, fragile-seeming home. . . . The entire setting [of the
> house] is wholly or . . . partially transparent.*
>
> (Miller 1961: 7)

Systems of setting and lighting are envisaged here as combining
to effect a radical differentiation of the house (small, frail,
transparent, in natural light) from its surroundings (tower-
ing, solid, opaque, reflecting an angry neon glow). At the
atmospheric level, the house may be viewed as a haven, a
retreat from reality: *'An air of the dream clings to the place'* (7).
It is a dream, however, environed by reality and, as such,
subject to threat. Symbolically, the stage picture stands as
a metaphorical condensation of the text's ideological preoc-
cupations. Willy Loman is an old-style travelling salesman,
rendered redundant by corporate capitalism. The fragility of
the house corresponds to the fragility of Willy's dream; the

externalisation of menace to a denial, to the 'low man', of the American Dream.

The action of *Death of a Salesman* modulates between present and past, between reality and fantasy. Miller's directions stipulate that *'whenever the action is in the present the actors observe the imaginary wall-lines, entering the house only through its wall at the left.'* This convention is breached for all other scenes, the characters entering or leaving a room *'by stepping "through" a wall to the forestage'* (7). The spectator is thereby furnished with a pictorial index of the location of the action.

For an example of the differential operation of discrete elements within a single stage picture, we return to the establishing stage directions of *Hedda Gabler*. The decoration and furnishing of the drawing-room have already been noted as signifiers of oppressiveness. In contradistinction, there is a natural light source: *'Morning light: the sun shines in through the glass doors.'* The doors give on to a veranda, and *'autumn foliage'*, and the room itself displays a profusion of flowers: *'All around the drawing-room are bouquets of flowers in vases and glasses; others are lying on the tables'* (263). The cultural connotations of sunlight and flowers are in general terms positive. The systems of lighting and, with regard to the flowers, properties would appear to be envisaged as operating at cross-purposes with the setting. The initial stage picture in *Hedda Gabler* is in consequence ambiguous to a high degree.

The orchard which gives *The Cherry Orchard* its name is a visible element in the stage pictures for Acts I, II and IV, and a significant absence from the Act III picture. It serves a range of functions, which will be examined further in the next section. It is of interest to the present discussion as a polyvalent symbol. Each of the main characters reflects on the significance which the orchard holds for her/him. For Liubov Andryeevna and for Gayev, it evokes a past made up of happier and more innocent times (347–8). For Ania, it constitutes a past from which she feels herself breaking away (367). For Trofimov, it connotes generations of serfdom (368), and for Feers the more productive 'old days', half a century before (344). For Varia, it signifies security at the price of drudgery (394), and for Lopahin, investment, productivity and his own rise in social standing (383–4).

149

STAGE PICTURE AND VISUAL METAPHOR

It is apparent from the preceding discussion of Miller's conception of the setting for *Death of a Salesman* and Crowley's designs for both setting and costume for *Hedda Gabler* that the stage picture may be invested with a symbolic currency. In both cases the dramatist has envisaged a single setting, albeit one which is highly complex and which offers discrete playing areas. In *The Cherry Orchard*, Chekhov's establishing stage directions for the setting of each of the four acts constitute the serial development of the individuated stage pictures into an overarching visual metaphor, which operates as a device wherewith both to counterpoint the play's narrative line and to foreground its ideological concerns.

With regard to the individual pictures Chekhov has, in Fergusson's terms, attributed to the settings 'a role which changes and develops in relation to the story' (1968: 167). The dramatist indicates his settings as follows:

> *ACT ONE A room which used to be the children's bedroom and is still referred to as the 'nursery'. There are several doors: one of them leads to* ANIA's *room. It is early morning: the sun is just coming up. The windows of the room are shut, but through them the cherry trees can be seen in blossom. It is May, but in the orchard there is morning frost.*
>
> *ACT TWO An old wayside shrine in the open country; it leans slightly to one side and has evidently been long abandoned. Beside it there are a well, an old seat and a number of old stones which apparently served as gravestones in the past. A road leads to* GAYEV's *estate. On one side and some distance away is a row of dark poplars, and it is there that the cherry orchard begins. Further away is seen a line of telegraph poles, and beyond them, on the horizon, the vague outline of a town, visible only in very good, clear weather.*
>
> *ACT THREE The drawing-room of the Ranyevskaias' house. Adjoining the drawing-room at the back, and connected to it by an archway, is the ballroom. A Jewish band, the same that was mentioned in Act II, is heard playing in the hall. It is evening; the candles in a chandelier are alight. In the ballroom a party is dancing the Grand-Rond.*
>
> *ACT FOUR The same setting as for Act I. There are no pictures on the walls or curtains at the windows; only a*

few remaining pieces of furniture are piled up in a corner, as if for sale. There is an oppressive sense of emptiness. At the back of the stage, beside the door, suitcases and other pieces of luggage have been piled together as if ready for a journey.

Each of the four stage pictures, in conjunction with relevant passages of dialogue, tells as it were its own story. The Act I setting was formerly a children's bedroom. It continues to be referred to as the 'nursery', even though there are no children among the dramatis personae, and so directs the attention of the reader/spectator both to past events (the childhood of Liubov Andryeevna and Gayev; the death of Liubov's young son) and to the childlike characteristics of Liubov and Gayev. A director interested in counterpointing the verbal references might well commission a nursery design. The cherry orchard is visible through closed windows, the trees in blossom are covered with an unseasonable frost (334). Act II, set in open countryside, widens the focus to include the social context of the narrative. In the foreground, the derelict and abandoned shrine and graveyard may be read as indices of the decline of religion and a break with the past. At the level of the action, the setting provides an incongruous location for an afternoon excursion. The distant townscape and the line of telegraph poles suggest urbanisation, and the changing pattern and pace of life to which the estate-dwellers will prove unable to adapt. Act III moves back to the interior of the house. A 'little dance' (360) is in progress in the candle-lit ballroom, a graphic illustration of the declining social status and loss of social role of the rural gentry: 'We used to have generals, barons and admirals dancing at our balls, but now we send for the post-office clerk and the stationmaster, and even they don't come too willingly' (Feers, 378). Offstage, in the town, the estate is put up for auction. At the close of the act Lopahin, the son of peasants and the play's representative of the rising mercantile class, identifies himself as the purchaser. Act IV returns to the 'nursery' setting of Act I, the piles of furniture and luggage connoting 'an oppressive sense of emptiness'. The structured contrast between the opening and closing stage pictures serves both to index emphatically the changed circumstances of the characters and to underpin a nexus of

151

intersecting binary motifs: spring/autumn; childhood/old age; optimism/pessimism; order/disarray; arrival/departure.

If we now review the four stage pictures as a series, having regard to the shifting representation of the eponymous orchard (a potent and polyvalent symbol, as has already been demonstrated), the metaphorical dimension of Chekhov's scenographic project is immediately apparent. In Act I the orchard is clearly visible. The May frost constitutes a sign of disruption: something is rotten in the estate of Ranyevskaia. In Act II the orchard is placed in the middle distance, further out of sight both literally and figuratively. The spectator's point of view is aligned with the family's diminishing capacity to retain the estate. In Act III the orchard is removed wholly from view. It changes hands in the offstage sale. In Act IV the orchard is again clearly visible. Lopahin is now in a position to act, in his own interest, on the advice he had vainly attempted to offer Liubov Andryeevna and her family (343). The final stage direction of the play is *'the sound of an axe striking a tree'* (398). The series is shown in Figure 8.1.

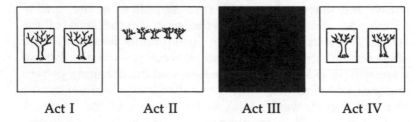

| Act I | Act II | Act III | Act IV |

Figure 8.1 The Cherry Orchard: serial development of stage pictures

In terms of the narrative line of *The Cherry Orchard*, the visual metaphor reflects the incapacity of Liubov and her family to make productive use of, and so to retain, the estate. In terms of the text's ideological agenda, it serves to underpin a recurrent concern with social change and with shifting class relations. To return, briefly, to the context of production, it might again be emphasised that the director and designer have much to gain from giving serious consideration to the directions for setting and other pictorial elements placed on offer by theatrically informed dramatists such as Chekhov, and much to lose from a cavalier disregard.

SOCIAL SEMIOTICS

It goes almost without saying that the spectator's reception of theatrical signs is informed, whether consciously or at a subliminal level, by her/his everyday experience of encoding and decoding analogous social signs; that one's response to setting, action, and the appearance and behaviour of the actor-in-role is in large measure the product of one's social experience and general cultural knowledge of, for example, domestic environments, social rituals, vestimentary codes, facial expression, body language and spatial relationships. Given that the social field is constituted by systems of relations between individuals and/or groups, and that theatrical representation (whether mimetic or abstracted in varying degrees) is concerned to mirror social interaction, it follows that the spectator will 'read' the theatrical in terms of the social.

Pierre Guiraud's examination of the codes that govern social communication and signification identifies four main categories of activity:

1 Protocols, which function to establish and regulate communication.
2 Rituals, which affirm 'the solidarity of individuals relative to religious, national or social obligations contracted by the community'.
3 Fashions, which assert, as fact or aspiration, membership of a specific group.
4 Games, representations of social reality within which participants are positioned to enact, and to experience affectively, aspects of that reality.

(1975: 92–8)

Guiraud offers two broad categories of social signs, concerned respectively with identity and with behaviour:

1 Signs of identity, which mark the individual as an adherent of a specific social group. Such signs include coats of arms, flag, totems etc.; uniforms; insignia and decorations; tattoos, make-up, hair-styles, etc.; names and nicknames.
2 Behavioural signs, which mark actual or desired relationships between individuals. Such signs include tone of voice; greetings and expressions of politeness; insults; kinesics; proxemics.

(ibid.: 84–90)

Guiraud observes that social signs are 'iconic in nature, and are related to aesthetic signs' (ibid.: 90), and it is immediately apparent that the spheres of activity and categories of sign noted above find point-for-point correspondence in theatrical representation. It is further apparent that the spectator's decoding of the stage picture is informed by the broad range of social experience: 'Seeing is never a mere reception; it anticipates and projects, in terms of what culture has taught' (Lowe 1982: 80).

Robert Hodge and Gunther Kress explore the ideological implications of spatial relationships, arguing for the physical interrelation of bodies in space as the 'most fundamental' dimension of the semiotic situation. They note the preponderance of linguistic formulations articulating social meaning through spatial terms (e.g. 'keeping one's distance', 'high status'), and suggest that, while such figures of speech are read metaphorically, what they in fact express is 'a basic equation between the ordering of bodies in physical space and the relationships between persons in social space' (1988: 52–3).

The work of the anthropologist Edward Hall is drawn upon both by Guiraud and by Hodge and Kress. Hall, who coined the term 'proxemic' to designate the category of meanings produced by physical relations in space (see Chapter 6), investigated the significance of distance in differential speech-acts. The relevance of such work to a semiotic study of the pictorial dimension of stage production is manifestly clear from Table 8.1, which identifies eight significant distances in terms of both denotation and connotation (Guiraud 1975: 89).

Two further points may be noted in passing. Firstly, social signs are both culturally and historically specific. Hall's work relates to the spatial conventions of *North* American speakers. While distance might be thought to be a function of acoustic necessity, it is to a significant degree determined by convention. As Guiraud observes, whereas English and North American speakers maintain a 'polite' distance, Latin Americans (for example) tend to reduce this: 'The result is that the former tend to feel constrained and attacked by the latter, who find them cold and distant' (1975: 88). As an example of historical specificity, one might cite the peacock finery and extravagant conventions of carriage, posture and gesture of the Restoration gallant (and his stage counterpart). In the second place, the proxemic sign tends towards complexity

Table 8.1 Proxemics and the speech-act

1. Very close (5 to 20 cm)	Slight whisper	Very secret
2. Close (20 to 30 cm)	Audible whisper	Confidential
3. Fairly close (30 to 50 cm)	Low voice indoors Full voice outdoors	Confidential
4. Neutral (50 to 90 cm)	Low voice, low intensity	Personal subject
5. Neutral (1.30 to 1.50 m)	Full voice	Impersonal subject
6. Public distance (1.60 to 2.40 m)	Full voice with slight emphasis	Public information intended for people other than person spoken to
7. Across a room (2.40 to 6 m)	Loud voice	Speaking to a group
8. Beyond these limits (from 6 to 30 m)	Loud voice	Greetings at a distance, departures, etc.

and ambiguity. For example, Hodge and Kress observe that closeness

> signifies a strong relationship which can either be posi-
> tive (love, intimacy) or negative (aggression, hostility).
> Closeness, on its own, thus carries a contradiction. It
> is a strongly ambiguous sign which is only disambigu-
> ated if there are other reasons or signs which control
> interpretation.

Finally, Hodge and Kress related the proxemic spectrum of distance/closeness, which operates on the horizontal axis, to the indexing of status (high/low) and power (possession/lack) on the vertical axis. It is by means of the interaction of the two 'axes of space', they argue, that ideological meanings are created (1988: 52–3).

THE PAINTING AS ANALOGUE

Whereas our knowledge of social codes and conventions, and hence our capacity to 'read' social signs, may to a considerable extent be assimilated reflexively as the consequence of membership of a particular society and exposure to its milieux and mores, knowledge of aesthetic codes and conventions tends to be acquired consciously, and in more formal circumstances.

In this section we shall argue that a compositional analogy is to be perceived between stage picture and painting, that stage pictures have been traditionally encoded in terms of the conventions of representation of realist art, and that the processes of decoding learnt for the purpose of 'reading' paintings are applicable equally to the stage picture.

With regard to the compositional analogy, it is apparent from the earlier discussion of the pictorial dimension of the work of Ibsen and Chekhov that the dramatist may envision in graphic detail both the dramatic environment and the characters that inhabit it. The development of a sequence of stage directions for setting, lighting, costumes and properties, and for the movement and grouping of characters, involves an imaginative process of composition analogous to that engaged in by the painter. This provokes, in both cases, a series of conscious, compositional choices in relation to the subject, attitude to subject, framing, arrangement of forms, line, colour, texture, and so on. In this capacity of picture-maker, the dramatist sets figures (characters) in a stagescape precisely as the painter may set figures (subjects) in a landscape.

We can adduce a nexus of symmetries and overlaps between the activities of painting and playwriting. Strindberg, in his preface to *Miss Julie*, acknowledges a debt to painting: 'As regards the décor, I have borrowed from the impressionist painters asymmetry and suggestion (i.e., the part rather than the whole), believing that I have thereby helped to further my illusion' (1976: 101). The focus on the trapped or traumatised individual in the work of Ibsen finds correspondences in the contemporary expressionist canvases of his compatriot, Edvard Munch. From the time of Inigo Jones, whose settings for the court masques of Ben Jonson introduced illusionistic stage design into England in the first decade of the seventeenth century (Womack 1986: 60), painters have worked in the theatre. Picasso also wrote plays. Brecht's use of the 'quotable gesture' (Benjamin 1973: 19–20) and his habitual fashioning of sharp visual contradictions suggest a painterly approach to the theatrical image, and it is significant that Benjamin describes epic theatre as proceeding 'by fits and starts, in a manner comparable to the images on a film strip' (1973: 21). Beckett's stage pictures are composed with an absolute precision, hard-edged images which, in the later plays, are revealed from darkness as though frozen in space and time, then animated until reclaimed by darkness. The recent Sondheim/Lapine collaboration, *Sunday in the Park with George* (National Theatre, 1990), was predicated upon the literal animation of a post-impressionist painting, Seurat's *Un dimanche après-midi à l'île de la Grande-Jatte* (Chicago Art Institute).

The encoding of the stage picture in the manner of realist painting may be seen as concomitant with the naturalistic project of mirroring an external reality on stage with photographic exactitude, a project which culminates in the theatre of Strindberg, Ibsen and Chekhov. As an artistic movement, realism occupied a dominant position in France throughout the second half of the nineteenth century. Its concern, in the words of the art historian Linda Nochlin, was to produce 'a truthful, objective and impartial representation of the real world, based on meticulous observation of contemporary life' (1971: 13).

One has only to reread the establishing stage directions of *Hedda Gabler* in the light of Nochlin's comment to be aware of a congruence of objectives between realist painting and naturalist stage design. The stage picture is 'framed' by the proscenium arch. Within the frame, the spectating eye is led from the drawing-room in the foreground to the inner room which occupies the background, from object to object in a circular tour of inspection, from the depicted stage environment to the offstage diegetic space of the garden. French windows are used to provide a 'natural' light source. The portrait of General Gabler, which overlooks the action from the rear wall of the inner room, both exerts a symbolic function (the iconic sign substituting for its absent referent) and operates, to use Anna Whiteside's term, as a 'self-referring artifact' (1988: 27), a painting within a 'painting'. Mention has been made of the sombre palette used to encode the stage picture's 'dark colours', 'autumn foliage' and 'thick carpet' (263).

With regard to the 'reading' of paintings, we learn to analyse composition; to assess the significance of the individual parts and of the relationship(s) between them. We learn to respond to formal and stylistic sign-posting, to register significant detail, and to identify and interrogate the encoding of the symbol.

Moreover, we learn to augment textual with ideological analysis, and in consequence to question our own practices of reading. Each of these processes has a clear application for the decoding of the stage picture. To offer a single example, we 'read' paintings as we read the printed page, from left to right. The audience left side of the stage is the 'strong' side, to which the eye of the spectator is regularly returned. Strong, i.e. dominant, entrances are therefore most effectively made from this side; weak, i.e. unobtrusive, entrances from the audience right side. A counterpointing convention has developed as a legacy of the raked stage. Strength, in these terms, may be compounded by the use of an upstage entrance; weakness, by the use of a downstage one.

The analogy with painting, while undoubtedly useful, may not be indefinitely pursued. The stage picture is subject to continual change, even where a setting is constant, through effects of lighting and through the movement of the actors. Moreover, as Womack notes, it is not possible for design and acting 'to approach the monolinear orientation of a painting' in all types of performance space (1986: 60). Where the proscenium arch functions as a picture-frame, the theatrical image is projected directly forward. Conversely, a performance in the round will shift its focus regularly, to accommodate, in turn, each section of the auditorium to the relative disadvantage of other sections.

ROLE OF SPECTATOR

In his article 'From Text to Performance', Pavis defines *mise-en-scène* as the 'confrontation of text and performance', the 'bringing together or confrontation, in a given space and time, of different signifying systems, for an audience'. He argues that *mise-en-scène* exists, as a structural system, 'only when received and reconstructed by a spectator from the production'. Hence, a function is attributed to the spectator in relation to the visual dimensions of production and performance: 'To decipher the mise en scène is to receive and interpret . . . as a spectator the system elaborated by those responsible for the production' (1988: 87). In Chapter 5, we posited a history of performance aesthetics broadly divided into three phases,

respectively characterised by the operations of conventionalism, by the cultivation of illusion and by the contestation
of illusionism. We shall conclude the present chapter with a
brief consideration of the role of the spectator in relation to
mise-en-scène, in terms of this three-phase model.

1. In contradistinction to the emblematic, and often highly
elaborate, scenography of the medieval stage, performance
in the open-air theatres of classical Athens and Elizabethan
London took place against a neutral, architectural background.
This background, the front wall of the stage-building or 'tiring
house' respectively, is assigned the identity of a given location
(or locations) according to the needs of the dramatic fiction.
Hence in *Oedipus the King*, the action is located before the
royal palace of Thebes. The Messenger's speech assumes, in
its recounting of the offstage violence, some sense of a palace
interior (235–7) on the part of the original spectators, as well
as the capacity to 'project' an image of the exterior on to the
stage-building. A fictional location is assigned also to the landscape beyond the theatre, the hills of Attica standing substitute
for Mount Cithaeron (183, 219, 224, 227, 243, 246).

In the Elizabethan public playhouse, the structure of the
building could be invested as required with characteristics
of a given location. In *Macbeth*, I.6, King Duncan and his
retinue arrive before the Macbeths' castle at Inverness. Duncan
conventionally identifies the new location, setting both scene
and atmosphere:

> This castle hath a pleasant seat; the air
> Nimbly and sweetly recommends itself
> Unto our gentle senses.

Banquo adds a symbolic dimension, and 'points out' specific
features of castle architecture which the spectator is invited to
imagine:

> This guest of summer,
> The temple-haunting martlet, does approve
> By his loved mansionry that the heaven's breath
> Smells wooingly here. No jutty, frieze,
> Buttress, nor coign of vantage, but this bird
> Hath made her pendent bed and procreant cradle.

(1–8)

(As for the casting of the martlet, there were, presumably, birds enough in the playhouse eaves.)

The spectator, then, is engaged in a project of creative collaboration, with the dramatist and actor, in the interest of a more complete realisation of the performance. With regard to costume, the richly imagistic language of *Antony and Cleopatra* positions the spectator to superimpose, upon the stage reality of a robed and painted boy, a version of the mythicised Cleopatra. In *As You Like It*, the Italianate disguise convention is elaborated to the extent that the boy actor playing Rosalind plays a girl who, disguised as a boy, takes the part of a girl to play the game of curing Orlando of love-sickness (Doebler 1974: 35). The role, and responsibility, of the spectator in the Elizabethan public playhouse is explicitly articulated in the prologue to Act I of *Henry V*:

> For 'tis your thoughts that now must deck our kings,
> Carry them here and there, jumping o'er times,
> Turning th'accomplishments of many years
> Into an hour-glass.

> (28–31)

The history of any period of theatre involves the history of the education of the spectator in particular habits of spectatorship. The more complex and sophisticated textual and performance conventions become, the greater the demand that is made on the spectator. In the theatres characterised by conventionalism, an active mode of spectatorship is offered. The spectator is invited to participate in the construction and operation of imaginative space, and to learn such conventions as will facilitate effective participation.

2. The mode of spectatorship placed on offer by illusionistic theatre is one of complicit passivity. The development of the 'fourth wall' convention, together with artificial lighting, and a blurring of the role/real boundary which led the actor and consequently the spectator to identify unproblematically with the character, worked to draw the spectator into the diegetic universe. The naturalist project of analogical representation at the levels of setting and dialogue would have produced, for the original spectators of *Hedda Gabler* (for example), a nexus of correpondences between stage picture and their own domestic environment, between character and their own circle

of acquaintance. Mayakovsky makes this point precisely in the prologue to the 1921 version of *Mystery-Bouffe*. In a gibe at Chekhov's *Uncle Vanya*, selected as representative of the bourgeois theatre now under attack, he reminds the spectators, 'uncles, aunts, you have at home'. Theatre, he insists in the course of a polemical and partial analysis, has cause to be more ambitious in its choice of objects and subjects (803–5).

3. We have noted that the anti-illusionistic aesthetic of dis-tanciation, which characterises the third phase of the history of theatrical performance, may in large part be read as a return to the convention-based modes of presentation of the first phase. Performance is now foregrounded *as* performance, and the spectator is again accorded an active role in the processes of meaning-production.

In both *The Mother* and *Top Girls*, *mise-en-scène* operates as an instrument of the ideological projects of the texts, directing the attention of the spectator from the respective representa-tions of class struggle and gender politics outwards to the social contexts. The orientation of *Endgame* is metaphysical rather than social. Here, *mise-en-scène* works to construct an affective level of response in the spectator, by aligning the latter's experience of production and performance with the characters' experience of the diegetic universe, and to provoke a questioning of that response. The metaphorical dimension of both setting and action provokes questioning also. The use of paradox and ambiguity in the work of Beckett, and the use of the dialectical method in work within the 'Brechtian' tradition, commission an active mode of spectatorship. The spectator is offered a task of work, and provided with the space (both literal and figurative) wherein to perform it.

9

TEXT IN PERFORMANCE

We propose in this chapter both to synthesise the semiotic readings of text and performance developed in this volume and to theorise stage practice in relation to a single play, Samuel Beckett's *Krapp's Last Tape* (1965 [1958]). The two performances we use are Patrick Magee's Royal Court performance (original staging 1958, filmed 1972) and the filmed performance of Jack MacGowran, which was lost for seventeen years, and only recently had its first screening in the posthumous season of tributes to Beckett (1990).

TEXT

Written a year later than *Endgame*, *Krapp's Last Tape* is a further example of Beckett's bleakly minimalist representation of the human condition. The knowable stage world is now reduced to a single 'wearish old man: KRAPP' and a tape-recorder, the action largely confined to the fragmentary playing-back of a diaristic recording made some thirty years before. Krapp is alienated from his younger self, a state of mind which might be read as a reluctance to accept his current intellectual and sexual deterioration.

With regard to form, *Krapp's Last Tape*, like *Endgame*, is composed in one act and opens with an extended sequence of mime which establishes the terms of the game to be played. The world of the 'radical' text is immediately signalled to the reader as the stage conventions of 'bourgeois' dramatic exposition are overturned. Where traditionally we have a sense of location, time and the beginnings of an action, here we are presented with 'Krapp's den', in which Krapp is seated at a table on 'a late evening in the future'. The signs of disruption which characterise the opening sequences are constant throughout the text which, 'radical' in form, refuses the structural conventions of act or scene divisions, unity of plot, etc.

Furthermore, the traditional use of an informational, interactive mode of dialogue, as the means of delineating character and advancing narrative in an opening sequence, here gives way to the alternation of solipsistic monologues between the 'I' present (Krapp at 69) and the 'I' past (Krapp at 39 on tape). The merest semblance of interaction between the two voices is found in old Krapp's despairing disavowal of his younger self. The text quite deliberately undermines the reader's habitualised capacity to extrapolate a coherent and unified character from the two Krapps. The disjunction between the 'I' present and the 'I' past constitutes the negation of a unified character history. Moreover the *Haupttext* is framed by a *Nebentext* which is detailed but confined to functionalistic directions. No indication is given here of character psychology or background.

PERFORMANCES

The space

Beckett's substantial extra-dialogic directions contain instructions for establishing the minimal set which constitutes 'Krapp's den'. Both performances locate the main area of stage action around Krapp's table, centre stage, in both instances circled with light from a pendulant lamp above the table (established in the intra-dialogic direction from the taped voice, 'the new light above my table is a great improvement': 12). Neither the minimalist interior which is visibly represented, nor the diegetic space to which Krapp frequently retires to drink or fetch the boxes of tapes, locates the spectator in a particular time, place, or setting. Like the seventeenth-century French Classical *palais à volonté*, which signifies the world of tragedy, the space is an undefined, nondescript vacuum, which *locates* the universe of the absurd.

Like the *palais à volonté*, Krapp's den also serves to denote the physical boundaries of the dramatic universe. Its confining qualities are, however, signified differently in the two performances. The den in Magee's performance is given a labyrinthine quality. The corridor perspective, created by Krapp's repeated long walks back through two framed doorways to the rear room-off, the irregular shaping of the main room, the play of light and darkness and the casting of a gigantic human shadow, combine to suggest a maze from which there is no exit. The offstage room is merely an extension of the room that is mimetically presented before us: no escape, simply more of the same. This is further reinforced by Magee-Krapp's movements in relation to the stage space: his feeling for the line of the wall, the use of touch to assist the failing eyes as he moves awkwardly backwards and forwards through the den.

On the other hand, MacGowran's Krapp is situated in a cell-like den with a curtained recess to which Krapp repeatedly retires. The sense of confinement is created through the use of darkness. The central light above Krapp's table gives way to a penumbral sphere, beyond which the edges of the den are lost. The brief sphere of light in which Krapp locates himself – 'With all this darkness round me I feel less alone. (Pause.) In a way. (Pause.) I love to get up and move about in it, then back here to . . . (hesitates) . . . me. (Pause.) Krapp.' (12) – is reinforced in MacGowran's performance by a cautious surveying of the pools of darkness.

Objects

Beckett's Nebentext offers a further set of directions for the use of objects in the stage space. These feature significantly in the opening mime. As is frequently the case in Beckett's plays, the tangibility of objects offers the characters a fleeting moment of reassurance in a world that is wholly intangible. The use of objects as an element of staging, in response to Beckett's instructions, is, however, executed quite differently in the two performances.

In MacGowran's performance objects acquire significance through a process of defamiliarisation. In the opening mime, which MacGowran pursues at length and in detail, Krapp negotiates a whole series of objects – watch, envelope, drawer, bananas, tapes, ledger and recorder. Each object presents a disproportionate amount of difficulty. The watch, envelope, ledger and tapes are hard to see. Opening the drawer requires a walk to the far side of the desk and the effort of reaching to the back of it to extract the second banana. The skin of the first banana trips him up, and the recorder, when fetched, presents an enormous hurdle in terms of the effort required to extract the lead and plug the machine into the lamp above.

The process of defamiliarising the objects established in the stage space is further achieved by distorting the sounds they make. The crashing and banging of objects is recorded in the performance so as to foreground their materiality, thereby achieving a disjunction between the sound and the object which made it, which further reawakens our perception of the object(s) brought into play. (A clear example is the creaking sound of the first tape wound on to the recorder.) Alternatively, as with the offstage uncorking of a bottle, the sound may replace the object. MacGowran's Krapp is located among these many inanimate objects in the stage space, whose sounds constitute the only, and therefore dominant, auditive sign-system during the course of the opening mime. The wordless Krapp, in this sequence, is decoded as part of the world of objects. MacGowran-Krapp's opening sigh, for example, is accompanied by a gesture of self-hugging (i.e. man as tangible object) and, as he negotiates the stage space, his shuffling footsteps leave a trail of disembodied sound.

In Magee's performance the abridged opening mime (the envelope and uncorking sequences are, for example, omitted) offers a different mode of object-play. Here, objects do not acquire the same degree of significance. Rather they are treated in accordance with their functional, material properties. It is not an extended game-play between actor, objects and space which dominates the opening sequence in this performance, but the proxemic dimension of actor–space relations. The silent picture is dominated not by sounds and objects, but by the feverish activities of Krapp which are centred (a) on the obsessional banana-eating and (b) on the preparations of the stage space for the business of listening. To this end, Krapp makes three hurried, awkward trips to fetch the tapes, the ledger and the recorder as preparation for the listening activity.

Actors

1 *Identity*: Both MacGowran and Magee are actors who bring to their performances a reputation as Beckett actors – whose repertoires, performance style and public identity link them

firmly to the dramatist and his theatre. In Magee's performance, the link between dramatist and actor is further strengthened by the fact that the play was written for him (Knowlson and Pilling 1979: 81). This was brought to the attention of the viewer in the voice-over introduction to the recent screening of the performance as part of the BBC2 *Wake for Sam* tribute (1990). The prefatory statement set up audience expectations immediately prior to the performance. This type of 'audience foreknowledge', as Dyer terms it (1979: 121–2), encodes viewer/spectator expectations, and here one might also cite the media coverage given to Beckett at the time of his death, the several tributes offered by both BBC2 and Channel 4.

2 *Appearance*: Also contained in Beckett's opening set of directions are precise instructions for the costuming and physical characterisation of the 'wearish old man: KRAPP'. While the vestimentary signs in both performances contribute to the image of the dishevelled, unkempt, failing Krapp, the respective physical appearances of the two actors also contribute their own (very different) signs to the picture of decline and disarray. The round, ruddy face of Magee, beaded with sweat, foregrounds the signs of Krapp the habitual drinker. MacGowran's large popping eyes, mass of unruly grey hair and thin physique ending in long, white, pointed shoes, tend rather to suggest a clown-like image of senility. Additional elements of decrepitude are built into the physical appearance of the two actors by conventional signs of ageing and self-neglect, such as the blacking-out of teeth, or, as in the case of Magee's Krapp, the heavily tobacco-stained fingers.

3 *Gesture*: The image of the 'wearish old' Krapp is further translated into sets of bodily and facial expressions, which foreground his hearing difficulties, short-sightedness and unsteady walk. Both performers encode their performances with sets of movements which establish Krapp's failing body: the listening positions at the side of the tape-recorder, the close peering at the ledger or cassette boxes, the shuffling (MacGowran) or agitated (Magee) walk to and from the table and the recess.

As this is a solo performance, and much of the 'action' is located around Krapp and his listening to the diaristic recording, there are further sets of gestures which signify a mode, however minimal, of interaction between Krapp present and his former, taped, self. In Magee's performance, the listening Krapp assumes a very still position in terms of head and body movement which connotes concentration. Signs of intense concentration are further encoded in the taut muscles of the face. Particular emotional responses are located chiefly in facial expressions created by the flickering of the eyes and trembling of the lips. These are accentuated by the relative stillness of the whole body and the close-up camerawork (see Table 9.1, pp. 170–4 for further details). The stillness of the listening mode is sharply contrasted with the sequences away from the table, which are dominated by an agitated, feverish mode of gesture; for example, the opening mime which functions as a preparatory sequence, setting up the main business of listening.

MacGowran's performance, on the other hand, draws more heavily on gestures which function as attitudinal markers both in relation to stage objects and to the taped self. When listening to the tape, MacGowran's Krapp responds with frequent nods or shakes of the head, a scratching of the head with his hand, a quizzical raising of the eyebrows or widening of the eyes, which signal attitudes of approval, disgust or bewilderment in relation to his former self. What is offered to the spectator is a series of gestural codes which visually mark Krapp's changes in attitude, emotional state, and so on. On the part of the performer, these are deduced intra-dialogically from the text. For example, MacGowran illustrates the lines 'A small, old, black, hard, solid rubber ball. (*Pause.*) I shall feel it, in my hand, until my dying day' (15) with the stretching out of his arm and opening of the hand to mime the holding of the ball. Similarly, in the reiterated recollection of the love-making sequence, the line 'I lay down across her with my face in her breasts and my hand on her' (17) is accompanied by MacGowran laying his head across the recorder and embracing the machine with his hands, physicalising the remembrance of love past. In contrast, Magee, in both of these sequences, simply intensifies the dominant mode of concentrated listening to indicate a state of highly charged emotion.

4 *Voice*: Krapp's spiralling decline is further signified in the vocal fragmentation of Krapp: the speaking voice present, commenting on and listening to the recorded voice past, comments on and listens to an even younger self. The use of a speaking voice in the present and the pre-recorded voice of the

past suggests that the performance offers a dual set of auditive signs generated by the actor, which replaces the traditional convention of the two-way, speaker–listener/listener–speaker interchange. Synthesis of the two auditive systems is rare and momentary, but found, for example, in the brief choruses of laughter, past uniting with present.

The unique 'cracked voice' of Magee, which had inspired Beckett's writing of the piece, and which gave rise to a stage direction (9), is central to his performance. His relatively contained gestic style as identified in (3) above, is a corollary of the dominance of the dual auditive sign-system generated by the actor. The minimal movement of the listening body throws greater emphasis on to the taped words. The 'cracked' timbre of Magee's speaking voice in the present is a further sign of Krapp the 'wearish old man'. The performance dynamic of, and tension in, Magee's playing is located primarily between the silent, listening Krapp present and the voice of Krapp past. The concentration and containment of the actor's visual sign-system contrasts with the dexterity, modulation and effusiveness of the actor's dual systems of auditive signs.

As MacGowran draws more heavily on the visual signs generated by the actor, notably in relation to gesture, so concentration on the auditive sign-system of the taped voice is displaced. The dominance of the visual sign-system centred on the actor makes an overriding demand on the spectator's attention. That said, MacGowran uses the voice of Krapp present to define an attitude to objects, in the process of naming them: 'Spooool!', stretched far beyond the doubled vowels, is virtually sung; 'Box' is barked. In keeping with this approach, a fuller use than in the Magee version is made of the non-verbal vocal noises ('Ah'; 'Hm') that recur in the opening monologue (10–11). In contrast to this playful linguistic mode – which constitutes, in Julia Kristeva's terms, an irruption of the semiotic into the symbolic order of discourse (1980: 124–47) – the taped voice of Krapp past is made businesslike, self-consciously 'authorial'.

CINEMATIC SIGNIFICATION

We now move to a detailed consideration of the differential approaches of McWhinnie/Magee and Schneider/MacGowran to the staging of Krapp's opening mime, and of the cinematic elements of camera position, shot and angle, and editing style, as additional and complementary systems of signification.

Beckett's establishing stage directions for the setting are as follows:

> *Front centre a small table, the two drawers of which open towards the audience. . . . On the table a tape-recorder with microphone and a number of cardboard boxes containing reels of recorded tapes. Table and immediately adjacent area in strong white light. Rest of stage in darkness.*
>
> (9)

With regard to the position and the design of the table, both productions take issue with the directions. Magee's table is angled slightly downstage audience right, and has one drawer only. MacGowran's is placed right of centre. In both cases, the drawer/s is/are at the right-hand side. The positional changes have clear implications for camerawork, as will be demonstrated. Both productions begin with the table-top bare. At the close of the sequence, Krapp *'goes with all the speed he can muster backstage into darkness. . . . He comes back into light carrying an old ledger. . . . He lays ledger on table . . .'* (10). Both productions pick up on this, ignoring the directions for a pre-set table and requiring Krapp to make two further journeys to fetch tapes (now contained in cake or biscuit tins) and tape-recorder. The order of fetching varies. Magee begins with the tins, then the ledger, and finally the tape-recorder. MacGowran reverses the order of ledger and tins. Repetition-with-difference is a constitutive element of Beckett's work (see Connor 1988), and the extension from one journey to three is wholly in keeping with the insistent plays on fumbling in pockets, business with keys, peering, and business with bananas commissioned by the stage directions. With regard to the stage picture, the McWhinnie/Magee production constructs a *trompe-l'oeil* geometric perspective, a light-and-shadow corridor for Krapp's forays into the inner room. The Schneider/MacGowran version conforms more closely to the given directions. The curtained doorway upstage audience left is barely visible until the curtain is drawn open. (The Tiffany lampshade strikes a somewhat incongruous note, and might be taken, along with the leather-backed chair, to connote a faded gentility.)

169

Table 9.1 is intended to serve two purposes. First it offers an indication of the extent to which Beckett's stage directions have been variously adhered to, deleted, changed or developed in the productions under consideration. It will be immediately apparent that Magee's performance is much the sparer, and that MacGowran's both adopts authorial directions more regularly and is developed in greater detail within the compass of a recognisably 'Beckettian' aesthetic. The second purpose of the table is to draw attention to the uses of camerawork and editing in the two productions, in relation to the preceding discussion of performance and stage picture. In both cases, considerable care would appear to have been taken to match the precision of dialogue and stage directions with a corresponding and appropriate technical precision.

Table 9.1 Krapp's Last Tape

Stage directions: opening mime	Magee/camera	MacGowran/camera
1 *KRAPP remains a moment motionless,*	A. Establishing shot: medium shot (MS).	F. Establishing shot: Long shot (LS) of entire set.
2 *heaves a great sigh,*	Zoom in slowly to close-up (CU):	G. Zoom in slowly to centre table, to medium close-up (MCU) H. CU: 3/4-profile screen R, looking out L.
3 *looks at his watch,*	watch held to face.	G. MS: Finds watch. H. CU: Peers at watch, replaces it.
4 *fumbles in his pockets,*		
5 *takes out an envelope,*		G. MS: Finds envelope. H. CU: Peers at envelope, replaces it.
6 *puts it back,* 7 *fumbles,* 8 *takes out a small bunch of keys,*		

170

Table 9.1 Continued

Stage directions: opening mime	Magee/camera	MacGowran/camera
9 raises it to his eyes,		
10 chooses a key,		
11 gets up and moves to front of table.	B. MCU: KRAPP at R of table.	G. MS: Moves to R end of table. Camera pans slightly R to accommodate.
12 He stoops,		
13 unlocks first drawer,		Opens drawer.
14 peers into it,		
15 feels about inside it,		Withdraws brown paper bag.
16 takes out a reel of tape,		Unpacks reel from box from paper bag. Sweeps bag and box to floor with hand.
17 peers at it,		H. CU: Peers at reel.
18 puts it back,		G. MS: Replaces reel, closes drawer.
19 locks drawer,		
20 unlocks second drawer,		Opens second drawer.
21 peers into it,		H. CU: Face, eyes closed, as hand probes drawer out of shot.
22 feels about inside it,		
23 takes out a large banana,	B. (Continuation of 11)	G. MS: Withdraws banana.
24 peers at it,		
25 locks drawer,		
26 puts keys back in his pocket.		
27 He turns, advances to edge of stage,	C. CU: shot slightly from below. KRAPP shuffles into shot from R.	Moves to front of table. Camera pans slightly to L to accommodate.
28 halts, strokes banana,	Stroking omitted, otherwise as stage directions up to and including (32).	H. CU: Places banana against face, strokes it. Delicately peels four strips of skin. Delicately holds banana between forefinger & thumb.
29 peels it,		

171

Table 9.1 Continued

Stage directions: opening mime	Magee/camera	MacGowran/camera
30 *drops skin at his feet,*		G. MS: Delicately lets skin fall.
31 *puts end of banana in his mouth and remains motionless, staring vacuously before him.*		H. CU: Tilts head back slightly to receive banana. Mock-sacramental image. Smiles into camera.
32 *Finally he bites off the end,*		Chomps with enthusiasm.
33 *turns aside and begins pacing to and fro at edge of stage, in the light, i.e. not more than four or five paces either way, meditatively eating banana.*	D. MS: Camera perpendicular to angled table, panning L & R with KRAPP.	G. MS: Camera static. KRAPP walks to & fro, before front edge of table. Banana skin visible throughout.
34 *He treads on skin, slips, nearly falls,*	C.U: (34–6) as stage directions.	(34–6) as stage directions.
35 *recovers himself,*		
36 *stoops and peers at skin*	Stoops out of shot. Rises, holding skin; contemplates, throws skin away.	
37 *and finally pushes it, still stooping, with his foot over edge of stage into pit.*		H. CU: Face horizontal, turned to camera. G. MS: Kicks skin away.
38 *He resumes his pacing,*	D. MS: Repeat of (33), panning L & R with KRAPP.	Movement resumed as at (33).
39 *finishes banana,*		
40 *returns to table,*		H. CU: L of table. KRAPP shuffles behind table,
41 *sits down,*		tracked by camera. Back to R end of table.
42 *remains a moment motionless,*	C. CU: facing R, brooding.	
43 *heaves a great sigh,*		
44 *takes keys from his pockets,*		

Table 9.1 Continued

Stage directions: opening mime	Magee/camera	MacGowran/camera
45 *raises them to his eyes,*		
46 *chooses key,*		
47 *gets up and moves to front of table,*	B. MCU: Repeat of (11). KRAPP at R of table.	
48 *unlocks second drawer,*		G. MS: Repeat of (20). H. CU: Repeat of (21).
49 *takes out a second large banana,*	B. (continuation of (47).	G. MS: Repeat of (23).
50 *peers at it,*		
51 *locks drawer,*		
52 *puts back keys in his pocket,*		
53 *turns, advances to edge of stage,*	C. CU: Repeat of (27–31) for (53–7). Skin thrown away R. Otherwise as stage directions.	H. CU: Repeat of (27–31) for (53–7). Considers what to do with skin, which is thrown well out L. Otherwise as stage directions, bar vacuousness.
54 *halts, strokes banana,*		
55 *peels it,*		
56 *tosses skin into pit,*		Remarks camera.
57 *puts end of banana in his mouth and remains motionless, staring vacuously before him.*		
58 *Finally he has an idea, puts banana in his waistcoat pocket, the end emerging,*	C. CU: Appears to throw banana away also.	G. MS: Pockets banana, as per direction.
59 *and goes with all the speed he can muster backstage into darkness.*	E. Long shot (LS) of empty set. KRAPP into shot, walks upstage and disappears into inner room.	F. LS of entire set. KRAPP wanders upstage, draws curtain, disappears into inner room.
60 *Ten seconds. Loud pop of cork.*		Unseen imbibing observed.

Table 9.1 Continued

Stage directions: opening mime	Magee/camera	MacGowran/camera
61 *Fifteen seconds. He comes back into the light carrying an old ledger and sits down at table.*	Reappears with tins under both arms. Walks downstage.	Reappears with ledger, stomps purposefully downstage.
62 *He lays ledger on table,*	B. MCU: Crosses to table. Deposits tins.	Drops ledger on table. Dust rises.
	The pattern of (59/61/62) is twice repeated, as KRAPP subsequently fetches the ledger & then the tape-recorder. There is brief business with the lead as the recorder is plugged into an unseen socket at ground level.	The pattern of (59/61/62) is twice repeated, as KRAPP subsequently fetches the tins, and then the tape-recorder. There is long and uncharacteristically fluid camerawork, as the recorder is plugged into the overhead light fitting.
63 *wipes his mouth, wipes his hands on the front of his waistcoat, brings them smartly together and rubs them.*	A. MCU: Sits at table. CU: Reads ledger, face just visible between piles of tins.	I. MCU shot slightly from above. KRAPP seated behind table, reads ledger in small space cleared for the purpose.

The McWhinnie/Magee version of the mime employs five camera shots:

(A) A medium shot which marks out the space of the fictional world, and which establishes Krapp, as per the stage direction, *'sitting at the table, facing front'* (9).
(B) A medium close-up which offers a side view of the table and of the drawer at the audience right end.
(C) A close-up on Krapp in front of the table.
(D) A second medium close-up which offers an angled view of the set as Krapp walks *'to and fro'* in front of the table (10).
(E) A long shot of the left side of the room.

A, B, C and E are shot from the point of view of the 'ideal' theatre spectator, i.e. as though the camera were placed in the centre of the stalls. For D, the camera is perpendicular to the angled table, panning to accommodate Krapp's movement and in consequence foregrounding the geometric play of light and shadow. This serves to produce an effect of disequilibrium, in the manner of German expressionist cinema (Eisner 1973: Ch. 3). The camerawork is relatively fluid overall, adjusting to Magee's walking, or stooping, in and out of shot. That said, the final sequence of the mime is formally patterned. The use of a static camera and the E/B bracket editing (alternation of paired shots) combine to impart a ritualistic quality to the 'setting-up' of the space. This is the more self-consciously cinematic of the two versions, as is further apparent in the proportionately greater use made of close-up shots. The relative emphasis placed upon Magee's face works to privilege character over action.

The Schneider/MacGowran version employs four camera shots:

(F) A long shot which, again, marks out the space of the fictional world and establishes Krapp at his table.
(G) A medium shot of the table, centre screen.
(H) A close-up on Krapp in front of the table.
(I) A medium close-up across the table-top.

In this version, the camera is aligned throughout with the 'ideal' spectator. The camerawork is markedly static, and the editing cuts crisply between shots. MacGowran remains within shot throughout. Predicated upon a basic strategy of G/H bracket editing, the approach here is more formally patterned than in the McWhinnie/Magee production. The overall effect, notwithstanding the use both of close-ups and, in the concluding sequence, fluid camerawork, is of the square-on recording of a stage production.

The Schneider/MacGowran version is of particular interest at the level of spectatorship. In the first place, MacGowran's performance is informed by the reiterated use of the verb-form 'peers' in the stage directions (Table 9.1: 14, 17, 21, 24, 36, 50). The directions require Krapp to raise '*a small bunch of keys . . . to his eyes*' (9). While this business is omitted, the gesture itself is retained and appropriated to the business with, for example, the watch, the envelope and the reel of tape. Moreover, it is emphasised by means of the close-up shot, so that the spectator's attention is focused upon Krapp's acts of looking. It goes almost without saying that the viewing experience of the spectator will be both more directed and more fully implicated in the diegetic experience of the character as a function of the mobilisation of the cinematic apparatus. Secondly, a degree of self-referentiality is further apparent in the acknowledgement of, and playing to, the camera on the part of MacGowran-Krapp. Beckett's characters frequently demonstrate a post-modernist awareness of their status as narrative or dramatic constructs (McHale 1987: 12–13), hence subverting the conventional terms of the reader/spectator–character relationship. This subversion is compounded by the address to camera. The theatre spectator is accustomed to direct address. Chorus-work, soliloquy and aside, breaking out of role are recurrent features of 'classic' and 'radical' texts. The cinema spectator, conversely, is habituated to a convention analogous to that of 'fourth wall' theatre. The narrative conventions of mainstream cinema develop from those of the nineteenth-century realist novel and the bourgeois dramatic text. Hence the implicit contract of cinematic spectatorship is breached by address to camera, a device which 'leaves a space for the spectator to enter and thereby complete the work' (Harvey 1982: 49).

One additional point might be made with regard to spectatorship, since the use of filmed versions of *Krapp's Last Tape* has placed the issue on our agenda. While cinematic spectatorship has been interrogated from a range of sociological and psychoanalytic perspectives, particularly during the 'moment' of the film studies journal *Screen* in the 1970s and early 1980s, comparatively little work has been done in relation to theatre. As the work already achieved, both theoretically and methodologically, in the sphere of film studies places on offer a range of potentially rewarding approaches, it is patently to our advantage to apply these to the conditions and processes of spectatorship in theatre. Perhaps this lack of investigation has arisen as a function of the divide between 'literary' and 'theatrical' projects noted in Chapter 5, as the negative consequence of which, drama studies inhabits a theoretically disunified field. Furthermore, semiotics, as a discipline, is accused of leaving society out of the frame (Shevtsova 1989: 23), and it may be that sociologists and semioticians could further collaborative links, in order to gain a fuller picture both of audience composition and of the role of the spectator in the production of meaning.

10

CONCLUSION:
THE WAY FORWARD?

Our aim throughout this book has been to provide the reader
with an overview of the semiotics of the dramatic text and
of theatrical performance. In the chapters relating to text, we
have sought to indicate those elements of the dramatic which
are receptive to a semiotic way of 'seeing': shape, character,
dialogue and directions. In Part II, where performance *per se*
is the principal object of enquiry, we have taken care neither
to lose sight of textual study nor to establish a clear divide
between text and performance. We have attempted to highlight
a sense of intertextuality between the signifying systems of the
written and the performed by including a second chapter on
stage directions and a chapter on stage picture and visual
metaphor, in order to investigate the implications for realisation
within a performance context of the dramatist's 'instructions'.
The comparative analysis of the two performances of *Krapp's
Last Tape* was a means of integrating all of these concerns, and
of constituting an appropriate methodological and theoretical
paradigm. This way of working is, in part, a response to the
comments with which Elam concluded his 1980 survey, where
he looked forward to the challenging possibilities of work that
might arise from a more unified field of dramatic and theatrical
semiotic study.

One way forward would be to pursue individually, on a
more detailed basis than this overview has permitted, the formal elements of textual encoding, through to their manifes-
tation in performance. There is scope for a full-length study
of stage directions in the contexts of text and performance,
or a detailed examination of the progress of dialogue as a
linguistic sign-system from page to production. In short, there

is a demonstrable need for further work on both actual and potential links between the two 'texts'. We are also conscious of being able to offer, in the space available, one chapter only which addresses the analysis of the text *in* performance. More work in this field would serve both to underline the benefits of a semiotic methodology for theatre studies and to increase our understanding of theatre as a signifying system.

There are several further aspects of the theatrical sign-system which would reward a semiotic investigation. Though the actor, as sign, featured prominently in the early work of the Prague School and in subsequent classifications of sign-systems, the very complexity of the actor's presence and its centrality to the systems of staging opens up additional areas of enquiry. An increased focus on the actor as the site of a two-way investigation of the text–performance relationship, given her/his crucial function of mediation between the two 'texts', would further our understanding of the dynamics of dramatic and theatrical discourse. In the light of current interest in women's theatre it is apparent that work remains to be done towards understanding the signification and role of gender in performance contexts. Certainly the move in women's theatre, indicated in Chapter 6, towards experimentation with the non-verbal has more to teach us about the poetics of gesture.

Through the adoption of an historic and generic range of texts we have indicated the ways in which a semiotic methodology may be employed to advance understanding of the evolution of drama and theatre. From an awareness of the directions for staging on offer in medieval play scripts, for example, we are able to develop our understanding of how the playing spaces for the period were organised and how these functioned. The use of the three-phase developmental model has, in a broad sense, helped to foreground the evolution of playing space, production convention and acting style. Through the deployment of this range of texts we have come to realise how much work might be done on texts from different historical periods in order to place on offer new ways of 'seeing' them. In France, where theatre semiotics has been more widely adopted than in Britain, a number of semiotic readings of French classical drama have been produced (see, e.g., Ubersfeld 1981; Pavis 1985b). Might not Shakespeare and Jonson, for example, benefit as much from work of this kind as Racine and Marivaux?

179

Of all the areas of study which might be defined as suitable for some future semiotic investigation, one which seems to us to be urgently in need of address is the role of the spectator. We have given attention, at various points in this book, to issues such as the involvement of the spectator in the process of theatrical communication, the reception of the theatrical sign, and the reading of the social and cultural coding of *mise-en-scène*. While post-structuralist enquiry has shifted the focus of analysis from encoding to decoding, from the text *per se* to text–'reader' relations, this work has still to be developed in respect of theatre. A semiotic theorisation of the decoding activity of the spectator is an essential undertaking. It is also likely to prove a difficult undertaking, since it is here that semiotics is faced with its own limitation, its openness to the charge of reductiveness due to a dominant (some would argue, an exclusive) interest in formal properties.

It is in the light of this observation that we wish to make our final comments. We have argued consistently for the benefits of the semiotic approach, and have attempted, precisely because of a national reluctance to take on board these benefits, to offer an accessible study of the field to a British readership. At the same time, we would stress that while we view the semiotic approach as a highly productive way of 'seeing' theatre, it is only *one* way. Through a self-reflexive critique, theatre semiotics may also show us where other approaches and disciplines might come into play, both to widen our scope of understanding and to indicate where its own methodological principles might be subject to questioning, and hence to change. The relatively recent attention given to the practice of decoding, for example, would seem to point toward an investigation of the production of meaning which is weighted in favour of performance, whereas the tasks and processes involved in spectatorship remain to be fully mapped out and interrogated.

Given the key semiotic findings we have documented, and these concluding comments, we hope to have shown both the work that has been done and the types of project which might be generated from that work. The field of theatre semiotics is in many respects still wide open for investigation, and our understanding of theatre as a sign-system is still nascent. The semiotic method has yet to fulfil its potential as a challenging and a highly rewarding approach to the study of drama and theatre.

FURTHER READING SUGGESTIONS

This select list offers suggestions for further reading in specific areas. Some references are additional to those in the main body of the text. Full details of all works are given in the bibliography.

GENERAL SOURCES

A broad overview of the field of structuralism and semiotics is to be found in Hawkes (1977).

Volumes which contain detailed bibliographies related to the field of theatre semiotics include: Pavis (1976), Elam (1980), Issacharoff and Jones (1988).

TEXT

Shape

Sections on dramatic structure are to be found in Pavis (1976), Veltruský (1977) and Esslin (1987). On the story/plot distinction and techniques of defamiliarisation see the formalist contributions collected in Lemon and Reis (1965) and Matejka and Pomorska (1971). See also Brecht (1964) on 'alienation' techniques. For a formalist analysis of plot applied to Renaissance drama see Pavel (1985). On exits and entrances in relation to structure in Greek tragedy see Taplin (1985).

Character

On narratology and character see Propp's pioneering study (1968). Actantial models are explained in Greimas (1983) and (1970). For a summary of Souriau's 'calculus' see Elam (1980:

181

127–31) or Greimas (1983: Ch. 10). On the application of actantial models to dramatic texts, Ubersfeld (1978) is highly recommended reading. Veltruský (1977) offers a chapter on 'dramatic characters' (Ch. 6). Psychoanalytical approaches are usefully explored in Eagleton (1983) and Wright (1984).

Dialogue

For an early semiotic analysis of stage dialogue see Veltruský (1977). Elam (1980) usefully integrates an explanatory section on speech acts (Ch. 5) into a more wide-ranging, sometimes difficult, analysis of the use of language in drama. For introductory pieces on speech-act theory related to literature (and including examples from dramatic texts), see Ohmann (1971) and (1973). Fowler (1986: Ch. 8) illustrates a discussion of speech acts with extracts from Osborne's *Look Back in Anger* and Beckett's *Waiting for Godot*. Full-length studies of stage dialogue are offered in Burton (1980), which adopts a sociolinguistic approach, and Kennedy (1983) which contextualises a study of the use of duologue in dramatic texts in an historic and generic framework.

Stage directions

A markedly underworked area. However, introductory sections on stage directions are offered in Hayman (1977) and Reynolds (1986), though these are far from analytical in approach. We would suggest Ingarden (1973) as a useful departure point with regard to the *Haupttext–Nebentext* distinction, which is referenced again in his appendix (1958). The distinction is taken up productively in Fischer-Lichte (1984) and somewhat unhelpfully in Esslin (1987). On intra- and extra-dialogic directions see Veltruský (1977: Ch. 4). An exception to this somewhat impoverished field is Issacharoff's classification of the 'main linguistic functions' of directions (1988). Stage directions as instructions for performance are explored in the context of a medieval script by Jones (1988).

PERFORMANCE

Theatre as sign-system

Contributions from the Prague School are collected in Matejka and Titunik (1976). For an overview of the Prague School contributions see Deák (1976). Introductory essays on theatre as a sign-system and its vocabulary include Barthes (1972), Eco (1977), Elam (1977), Bassnett (1980) and Pavis (1981b). For classifications of sign-systems see Kowzan (1968) and (1975); Pavis (1976) and (1985a).

Actor

(1) See Veltruský's seminal essay (1964) and Honzl (1976). The actor as celebrity is discussed in Quinn (1990) and the concept of star and performer in the field of film is explored by Dyer (1979). Actor/text dynamics are raised in Gourville (1977).

(2) Actor and gesture: On the problems of reading gesture see Pavis (1981a), also reproduced in a section devoted to gesture in Pavis (1985b). On eastern theatre and gesture see Artaud (1974) and Brusak (1976). An analysis of gesture related to early Ibsen productions is offered in Cima (1983). Brecht's notion of *gestus* is widely discussed, but see, for example, Brecht (1964).

(3) Actor and space: On proxemic relations see Hall (1966), which underpins Guiraud (1975) and Hodge and Kress (1988). On *proxemics* and theatre, see Elam (1980, Ch. 3) for an overview.

Stage

(1) Space: An historic overview of the architectural developments of the stage space and theatre buildings is documented in Leacroft and Leacroft (1984). A semiotic approach to theatrical space is offered in Ubersfeld (1978: Ch. 4), and Pavis (1985b) offers a reading of the use of space in Marivaux's *Les Fausses Confidences* accompanied by production illustrations. The use of space is further considered, from a directorial perspective, in Schechner (1988a) and (1988b).

(2) Design: An analytical and well-illustrated account of Neher's work, particularly for Brecht, is offered in Willett (1986). Goldberg (1988) is a useful and well-illustrated volume, on design in relation to Performance Art. Ackermann *et al.* (1987) offers good illustrative material and effectively demonstrates the current state of British design. It is, however, weak on commentary and does not attempt analysis. Taylor (1982) pursues the links between stage picture and fine art.

Text/performance contexts

The dynamics between a dramatic text and its representation figure largely in semiotic studies of drama and theatre. Useful discussion on this point is to be found in Veltruský (1976), Kaisergruber (1977) and Pavis (1988).

Performance texts

There are relatively few semiotic readings of actual performances. For exceptions see the production analysis in Kowzan (1976), section five of Pavis (1985b) which offers readings of three productions, and Alter (1988) on Mnouchkine's 1982 production of *Richard II*.

Spectator

The spectator's role in the production of meaning is explored in the context of theatrical communication by Elam (1980, 1988). See also section six in Pavis (1985b), which is devoted to production and reception.

Issues of spectatorship have been interrogated and theorised to a conspicuously greater extent in the field of Film Studies. Useful introductions are provided by Ellis (1982), Kaplan (1983) and Penley (1988). Mulvey (1975) on the 'masculinisation' of the spectator position, which integrates institutional, psychoanalytic and semiotic approaches, has proved seminal; Mulvey (1989) includes this and subsequent, related articles. Alternative models are offered by Doane (1982, 1984) and de Lauretis (1984). An effective overview of recent work in the area is Stacey (1987). Dyer (1982) and Neale (1983) address masculinity as spectacle.

BIBLIOGRAPHY

The first date is that of the edition cited in the text. Date of first publication is given in square brackets. If context requires it, both dates are given in the text as well.

Ackermann, B., Blake, J., Craig, R., Don, R., Gastanbide, A. and Howard, P. (eds) (1987) *British Theatre Design 1983–1987*, Faringdon: Twynam Publishing.

Alter, J. (1988) 'Decoding Mnouchkine's Shakespeare (A Grammar of Stage Signs)', in Issacharoff and Jones, pp. 75–85.

Anon. (1956 [1909]) *Everyman*, in *Everyman and Medieval Miracle Plays*, ed. A.C. Cawley, revised edition, London: Dent.

Aristophanes (1964) *'The Frogs' and Other Plays*, trans. David Barrett, Harmondsworth: Penguin.

Aristotle (1965) 'On the Art of Poetry', in *Aristotle Horace Longinus*, Harmondsworth: Penguin Classics, pp. 31–75.

Artaud, A. (1974 [1938]) *The Theatre and its Double*, trans. Victor Corti, in *Collected Works*, vol. 4, London: Calder & Boyars.

Barker, C. (1977) *Theatre Games*, London: Methuen.

Barthes, R. (1968 [1964]) *Elements of Semiology*, trans. Annette Lavers and Colin Smith, London: Jonathan Cape; New York: Hill & Wang.

—— (1972 [1963]) 'Literature and Signification', in *Critical Essays*, trans. R. Howard, Evanston: Northwestern University Press, pp. 261–79.

—— (1975 [1970]) *S/Z*, trans. Richard Miller, London: Jonathan Cape; New York: Hill & Wang.

—— (1976 [1973]) *The Pleasure of the Text*, trans. Richard Miller, New York: Hill & Wang (1975); London: Jonathan Cape.

—— (1977) *Image, Music, Text*, essays selected and trans. Stephen Heath, London: Fontana; New York: Hill & Wang.

Bartlett, N. (1990) *Three Plays: Berenice, Le Misanthrope, The School for Wives*, Bath: Absolute Press.

Bassnett, S. (1980) 'Introduction to Theatre Semiotics', *Theatre Quarterly*, 38: 47–53.

—— (1984) Contributions to 'Semiotics and the Theatre: 1983 Alsager Seminar', *Interface*, 2.

185

Beckett, S. (1958) *Endgame*, London: Faber.
—— (1965 [1958]) *Krapp's Last Tape and Embers*, London: Faber.
Belsey, C. (1980) *Critical Practice*, London: Methuen.
Benjamin, W. (1973) *Understanding Brecht*, London: New Left Books.
Bentley, E. (1964) *The Life of the Drama*, London: Methuen.
Bogatyrev, P. (1976 [1938]) 'Semiotics in the Folk Theatre', in Matejka and Titunik, 33–50.
Braddon, M.E. (1985 [1862]) *Lady Audley's Secret*, London: Virago.
Bradley, A.C. (1961 [1904]) *Shakespearean Tragedy*, London: Macmillan.
Braun, E. (1982) *The Director and the Stage*, London: Methuen.
Brecht, B. (1964) *Brecht on Theatre*, trans. and notes, J. Willett, London: Methuen.
—— (1965) *The Messingkauf Dialogues*, trans. J. Willett, London: Methuen.
—— (1978 [1957]) *The Mother*, trans. Steve Gooch, London: Methuen.
Brook, P. (1968) *The Empty Space*, Harmondsworth: Penguin.
Brown, J.R. (1972) *Theatre Language*, London: Allen Lane/Penguin Press.
Brusak, K. (1976 [1939]) 'Signs in the Chinese Theatre', in Matejka and Titunik.
Burgin, V., Donald, J. and Kaplan, C. (eds) (1986) *Formations of Fantasy*, London and New York: Methuen.
Burton, B. (1980) *Dialogue and Discourse*, London: Routledge & Kegan Paul.
Campbell, P. (1922) *My Life and Some Letters*, London: Hutchinson.
Chekhov, A. (1959 [1904]) *The Cherry Orchard*, in *Plays*, trans. E. Fen, Harmondsworth: Penguin.
Churchill, C. (1984 [1982]) *Top Girls*, revised edition, London: Methuen.
Cima, G.G. (1983) 'Discovery Signs: The Emergence of the Critical Actor in Ibsen', *Theatre Journal*, March: 5–22.
Coe, R.N. (1964) *Beckett*, Edinburgh and London: Oliver & Boyd.
Cole, T. (ed.) (1960) *Playwrights on Playwriting*, London: MacGibbon & Kee.
Coleridge, S.T. (1907) *Biographia Literaria*, ed. J. Shawcross, 2 vols, Oxford: Oxford University Press.
Connor, S. (1988) *Samuel Beckett: Repetition, Theory and Text*, Oxford: Basil Blackwell.
Deák, F. (1976) 'Structuralism in Theatre: The Prague School Contribution', *The Drama Review*, 20: 83–94.
De Lauretis, T. (1984) *Alice Doesn't: Feminism, Semiotics, Cinema*, London: Macmillan.
Devereux, G. (1970) 'The Psychotherapy Scene in Euripides' Bacchae', *Journal of Hellenic Studies*, 90: 35–48.
Diderot, D. (1957 [1830]) *The Paradox of Acting*, trans. W.H. Pollock, New York: Hill & Wang.
Doane, M.A. (1982) 'Film and the Masquerade: Theorising the Female Spectator', *Screen*, 23(3–4): 74–87.
—— (1984) 'The Woman's Film: Possession and Address', in M.A. Doane, P. Mellencamp and L. Williams, *Revision*, Los

Angeles: American Film Institute/University Publications of America, pp. 67–82.

Doebler, John (1974) *Shakespeare's Speaking Pictures*, Albuquerque: University of New Mexico Press.

Donald, J. (ed.) (1983) *Formations of Pleasure*, London: Routledge & Kegan Paul.

Dover, K.J. (1972) *Aristophanic Comedy*, Berkeley and Los Angeles: University of California Press.

Dyer, R. (1979) *Stars*, London: BFI Publishing.

—— (1982) 'Don't Look Now – The Male Pin-Up', *Screen*, 23(3–4): 61–73.

Eagleton, T. (1983) *Literary Theory: An Introduction*, Oxford: Basil Blackwell.

—— (1986) *William Shakespeare*, Oxford: Basil Blackwell.

Eco, U. (1977) 'Semiotics of Theatrical Performance', *The Drama Review*, 21: 107–17.

—— (1979) *The Role of the Reader*, London: Hutchinson.

Eisner, L.H. (1973) *The Haunted Screen*, London: Secker & Warburg.

Elam, K. (1977) 'Language in the Theater', *Sub-Stance*, 18–19: 139–62.

—— (1980) *The Semiotics of Theatre and Drama*, London: Methuen.

—— (1988) 'Much Ado About Doing Things With Words (and Other Means): Some Problems in the Pragmatics of Theatre and Drama', in Issacharoff and Jones, pp. 39–58.

Ellis, J. (1982) *Visible Fictions*, London and New York: Routledge.

Esslin, M. (1987) *The Field of Drama*, London: Methuen.

Feldstein, R. and Sussman, H. (1990) *Psychoanalysis and . . .*, New York and London: Routledge.

Ferguson, J. (1972) *A Companion to Greek Tragedy*, Austin and London: University of Texas Press.

Fergusson, F. (1968 [1949]) *The Idea of a Theater*, Princeton: Princeton University Press.

Ferris, L. (1990) *Acting Women: Images of Women in Theatre*, London: Macmillan.

Fischer-Lichte, E. (1984) 'The Dramatic Dialogue – Oral or Literary Communication?', in Herta Schmid and Aloysius Van Kesteren (eds), *Semiotics of Drama and Theatre: LLSEE*, vol. 10, Amsterdam and Philadelphia: John Benjamin, pp. 137–73.

Fowler, R. (1986) *Linguistic Criticism*, Oxford: Oxford University Press.

Freud, S. (1985 [1916]) 'Some Character-Types met with in Psychoanalytic Work', in A. Dixon (ed.), The Pelican Freud Library, vol. 14, *Art and Literature*, Harmondsworth: Penguin.

Frye, N. (1971 [1957]) *Anatomy of Criticism*, Princeton: Princeton University Press.

Garvin, P.L. (1964) *A Prague School Reader on Esthetics, Literary Structure, and Style*, Washington: Georgetown University Press.

Gaskell, R. (1972) *Drama and Reality*, London: Routledge & Kegan Paul.

Goldberg, R.L. (1988 [1979]) *Performance: Live Art 1909 to the Present*, revised as *Performance Art: From Futurism to the Present*, London: Thames & Hudson.

Gourville, Y. (1977) 'The Actor-In-Project', *Sub-Stance*, 18–19: 121–9.

Greimas, A.J. (1970) *Du sens*, Paris: Seuil.

────── (1983 [1966]) *Structural Semantics*, trans. D. McDowell, R. Schleifer and A. Velie, Lincoln and London: University of Nebraska Press.

Grice, H.P. (1967) 'Logic and Conversation', in Peter Cole and Jerry L. Morgan (eds), *Syntax and Semantics: vol. 3: Speech Acts*, New York, San Francisco and London: Academic Press, pp. 41–58.

Griffiths, S. (1982) *How Plays are Made*, London: Heinemann.

Guiraud, P. (1975) *Semiology*, London: Routledge & Kegan Paul.

Hall, E. (1966) *The Hidden Dimension*, New York: Doubleday.

Hammond, B. (1984) 'Theatre Semiotics: An Academic Job Creation Scheme?', in 'Semiotics and the Theatre: 1983 Alsager Seminar', *Interface*, 2: 78–89.

Harrison, J.E. (1951 [1913]) *Ancient Art and Ritual*, London: Oxford University Press.

Harvey, Sylvia (1982) 'Whose Brecht? Memories for the Eighties', *Screen*, 23(1): 45–59.

Hawkes, T. (1977) *Structuralism and Semiotics*, London: Methuen.

Hayman, R. (1977) *How to Read a Play*, London: Methuen.

Hazlewood, C.H. (1972 [1863]), *Lady Audley's Secret*, in G. Rowell (ed.), *Nineteenth Century Plays*, 2nd edition, Oxford and New York: Oxford University Press.

Heinemann, M. (1985) 'How Brecht read Shakespeare', in Jonathan Dollimore and Alan Sinfield (eds), *Political Shakespeare*, Manchester: Manchester University Press, pp. 202–30.

Hodge, R. and Kress, G. (1988) *Social Semiotics*, Cambridge: Polity Press.

Honzl, J. (1976 [1940]) 'Dynamics of the Sign in the Theater', in Matejka and Titunik, pp. 74–93.

Horace (1965) 'On the Art of Poetry', in *Aristotle Horace Longinus*, Harmondsworth: Penguin, pp. 79–95.

Ibsen, H. (1950 [1890]) *Hedda Gabler*, in *Hedda Gabler and Other Plays*, trans. U. Ellis-Fermor, Harmondsworth: Penguin.

Ingarden, R. (1973 [1931]) *The Literary Work of Art*, 3rd edition, trans. G.G. Grabowicz, Evanston: Northwestern University Press. Includes Appendix (1958) 'The Functions of Language in the Theater', 1973: 377–96.

Ionesco, E. (1963) *Exit the King*, in *Plays*, vol. 5, trans. Donald Watson, London: John Calder.

Issacharoff, M. (1981) 'Space and Reference in Drama', *Poetics To-day* 2, 3: 211–24.

────── (1988) 'Stage Codes', in Issacharoff and Jones, pp. 59–74.

Issacharoff, M. and Jones, R.F. (eds) (1988) *Performing Texts*, Philadelphia: University of Pennsylvania Press.

Jones, R.F. (1988) 'A Medieval Prescription for Performance: *Le Jeu d'Adam*, in Issacharoff and Jones, pp. 101–15.

Kaisergruber, D. (1977) 'Reading and Producing Theatre', *Sub-Stance*, 18–19: 163–71.

188

Kaplan, E.A. (1983) *Women and Film: Both Sides of the Camera*, New York and London: Methuen.

Kellaway, K. (1989) 'A Space for Truth and Wit', *The Observer*, 5 March.

Kelsall, M. (1985) *Studying Drama: An Introduction*, London: Edward Arnold.

Kennedy, A.K. (1983) *Dramatic Dialogue: The Duologue of Personal Encounter*, Cambridge: Cambridge University Press.

Knowlson J. and Pilling, J. (1979) *Frescoes of the Skull*, London: John Calder.

Kowzan, T. (1968) 'The Sign in the Theater', *Diogenes*, 61: 52–80.

—— (1975) *Littérature et spectacle*, The Hague and Paris: Mouton.

—— (1976) *Analyse sémiologique du spectacle théâtral*, Lyon: Centre d'Etudes et de Recherches Théâtrales, Université Lyon II.

Kristeva, J. (1980) *Desire in Language*, ed. L.S. Roudiez, New York: Columbia University Press.

Lakoff, R. (1975) *Language and Woman's Place*, New York and London: Harper Colophon.

Leacroft, R. and Leacroft H. (1984) *Theatre and Playhouse*, London: Methuen.

Lemon, L.T. and Reis, M.J. (eds and trans.) (1965) *Russian Formalist Criticism: Four Essays*, Lincoln: University of Nebraska Press.

Liddell and Scott (1966) *Greek–English Lexicon*, Oxford: Oxford University Press.

Lowe, D.M. (1982) *History of Bourgeois Perception*, Brighton: Harvester.

Lyman, J. (ed.) (1976) *Perspectives on Plays*, London: Routledge & Kegan Paul.

McHale, B. (1987) *Postmodernist Fiction*, New York and London: Methuen.

Maeterlinck, M. (1899) 'The Tragical in Daily Life', in *The Treasure of the Humble*, London: George Allen; New York: Dodd, Mead, pp. 97–119.

Matejka, L. and Pomorska, K. (eds) (1971) *Readings in Russian Poetics: Formalist and Structuralist Views*, Cambridge, Mass.: MIT Press.

—— and Titunik, I.R. (eds) (1976) *Semiotics of Art: Prague School Contributions*, Cambridge, Mass.: MIT Press.

Maur, K. von (1982) *Oskar Schlemmer*, Munich: Prestel-Verlag.

Mayakovsky, V. (1960 [1921]) *Mystery-Bouffe*, second version, trans. G. Noyes and A. Kaun, in Noyes, pp. 801–81.

Miller, A. (1961) *Death of a Salesman*, Harmondsworth: Penguin.

Mulvey, L. (1975) 'Visual Pleasure and Narrative Cinema', *Screen*, 16(3): 6–18.

—— (1989) *Visual and Other Pleasures*, London: Macmillan.

Murray, G. (1965 [1918]) *Euripides and his Age*, London: Oxford University Press.

Neale, S. (1983) 'Masculinity as Spectacle', *Screen*, 24(6), 2–16.

Nochlin, L. (1971) *Realism*, Harmondsworth: Penguin.

Noyes, G. (1960) *Masterpieces of the Russian Drama*, vol. 2, New York: Dover.

Ohmann, R. (1971) 'Speech, Action, and Style', in Seymour Chatman (ed.), *Literary Style: A Symposium*, London and New York: Oxford University Press, pp. 241–54.

—— (1973) 'Literature as Act', in Seymour Chatman (ed.), *Approaches to Poetics*, London and New York: Columbia University Press, pp. 81–107.

Pavel, T.G. (1985) *The Poetics of Plot: The Case of English Renaissance Drama*, vol. 18 in 'Theory and History of Literature' series, Manchester: Manchester University Press.

Pavis, P. (1976) *Problèmes de sémiologie théâtrale*, Quebec: Quebec University Press.

—— (1981a) 'Problems of a Semiology of Theatrical Gesture', *Poetics Today*, 2(3): 65–93.

—— (1981b) 'Semiology and the Vocabulary of Theatre', *Theatre Quarterly*, 40: 74–8.

—— (1985a) 'Theatre Analysis: Some Questions and a Questionnaire', *New Theatre Quarterly*, 1(2): 208–12.

—— (1985b) *Voix et images de la scène*, revised edition, Lille: Lille University Press.

—— (1988) 'From Text to Performance', in Issacharoff and Jones, pp. 86–100.

Penley, C. (ed.) (1988) *Feminism and Film Theory*, New York and London: Routledge/BFI Publishing.

Pirandello, L. (1954 [1921]) *Six Characters in Search of an Author*, trans. F. May, London: Heinemann.

Propp, V. (1968 [1928]) *Morphology of the Folktale*, trans. and revised edition, Austin and London: University of Texas Press.

Quinn, M.L. (1990) 'Celebrity and the Semiotics of Acting', *New Theatre Quarterly*, 22: 154–61.

Racine, J. (1963) *Phaedra*, in *Phaedra and Other Plays*, trans. J. Cairncross, Harmondsworth: Penguin.

Rea, K. (1989) *A Better Direction*, London: Calouste Gulbenkian Foundation.

Reynolds, P. (1986) *Drama: Text into Performance*, Harmondsworth: Penguin.

Rimmon-Kenan, S. (ed.) (1987) *Discourse in Psychoanalysis and Literature*, London and New York: Methuen.

Saussure, F. de (1974 [1915]) *Course in General Linguistics*, trans., London: Fontana.

Schechner, R. (1988a [1977]) *Performance Theory*, revised edition, London: Routledge.

—— (1988b) 'Performance Orientations in Ritual Theatre', in Issacharoff and Jones, pp. 116–37.

Searle, J.R. (1969) *Speech Acts: An Essay in the Philosophy of Language*, Cambridge: Cambridge University Press.

—— (1971) *The Philosophy of Language*, London: Oxford University Press.

—— (1975) 'A Taxonomy of Illocutionary Acts', in K. Gunderson (ed.), *Language, Mind and Knowledge*, Minneapolis: University of Minnesota Press, pp. 344–69.

Segre, C. (1974) 'La funzione del linguaggio ne *L'Acte sans paroles* di S Beckett', in *Le strutture e il tempo*, Turin: Einaudi, pp. 253–74, cited Elam (1980).

Shakespeare, W. (1975) *As You Like It*, Arden edition, London: Methuen.

Shevtsova, M. (1989) 'The Sociology of the Theatre, Part One: Problems and Perspectives', *New Theatre Quarterly*, 5(17): 23–35.

Shklovsky, V. (1965a [1917]) 'Art as Technique', in Lemon and Reis, pp. 3–24.

—— (1965b [1921]) 'Sterne's *Tristam Shandy*: Stylistic Commentary', in Lemon and Reis, pp. 25–57.

Silverman, K. (1983) *The Subject of Semiotics*, New York: Oxford University Press.

Sophocles (1984 [1982]) *Oedipus the King*, in *The Three Theban Plays*, trans. R. Fagles, revised edition, Harmondsworth: Penguin.

Stacey, J. (1987) 'Desperately Seeking Difference', *Screen*, 28(1): 48–61.

Stanton, S.S. (ed.) (1957) *Camille and Other Plays*, New York: Hill & Wang.

Strindberg, A. (1976 [1964]) Preface to *Miss Julie*, trans. Michael Meyer, in Strindberg, *Plays*, London: Eyre Methuen, pp. 91–103.

Styan, J.L. (1971 [1965]) *The Dramatic Experience*, London and New York: Cambridge University Press.

Taplin, O. (1985 [1978]) *Greek Tragedy in Action*, revised edition, London: Methuen.

Taylor, P. (1982) 'Self and Theatricality: Samuel Beckett and Vito Acconci', *Art and Text*, 5: 2–11.

Todorov, T. (1973) 'Artistic Language and Ordinary Language', *The Times Literary Supplement*, 5 October.

Tynan, K. (1955) Review of Beckett's *Waiting for Godot*, *The Observer*, 7 August.

Ubersfeld, A. (1978) *Lire le théâtre*, Paris: Editions Sociales.

—— (1981) 'The Space of *Phèdre*', *Poetics Today*, 2(3): 201–10.

Veltruský, J. (1964 [1940]) 'Man and Object in the Theater', in Garvin, pp. 83–91.

—— (1976 [1941]) 'Dramatic Text as Component of Theater', in Matejka and Titunik, pp. 94–117.

—— (1977) 'Drama as Literature', *Semiotics of Literature 2*, PJR Press.

Whiteside, A. (1988) 'Self-referring Artifacts', in Issacharoff and Jones, pp. 27–38.

Wilde, O. (1988 [1895]) *The Importance of Being Earnest*, in *The Complete Plays*, London: Methuen, pp. 212–99.

Willett, J. (1986) *Casper Neher: Brecht's Designer*, London: Methuen.

Wilson, E. (1976) *The Theater Experience*, New York: McGraw-Hill.

Womack, P. (1986) *Ben Jonson*, Oxford: Basil Blackwell.

Wright, E. (1984) *Psychoanalytic Criticism: Theory in Practice*, London and New York: Methuen.

Young, R. (1981) *Untying the Text: A Post-Structuralist Reader*, London: Routledge & Kegan Paul.

Zich, O. (1931) *The Esthetics of Dramatic Art*, Prague: Melantrich.

INDEX

absence, significant 121–2, 149
absurd, the 68, 163
Ackermann, Belinda 183
actant 7, 41; spectator as 113;
  actantial model 10, 37–41,
  181–2; actantial role 41–2
acting 110; anti-emotionalist
  theory of 103, 118;
  conventions 11; emotionalist
  118; gestic 119, 121; history
  of 117–20; 'inner' 48; and
  language 58; 'method' 103;
  picture 118; social 47;
  style 179
action, dramatic 52, 53, 60, 65,
  77, 117, 129, 132, 140, 153, 161,
  162; actions 59, 126–7, 128,
  129–30
actor 7, 73, 91, 105, 110, 116–20,
  123, 125–31, 141, 158, 160,
  165–8, 183; boy 160; Brechtian
  47; and character 46–8, 153;
  as demonstrator 104; as icon
  6; linked to dramatist 165–6;
  machine as 46; narrative
  function of 21; puppet as 46;
  as scenic sign 101, 102–5, 141,
  179; as site of interdependent
  sign-systems 102, 105; social
  function of 104; Stanislavskian
  47; as structural unit 19;
  training of 46–7, 91, 118
actorial function 42; actorial
  role 41

actor–spectator configurations
  115–16
address, direct 35, 130, 176; to
  camera 176
Aeschylus 142; *Eumenides* 142
agora 113
alazon 60
alienation/distanciation/
  verfremdungseffekt 7, 32, 92,
  161, 181
Almeida Theatre, the 145
Alter, Jean 184
androgyny 48
Anouilh, Jean 20; *Antigone* 20
Apollinaire, Guillaume 48; *The
  Breasts of Tiresias* 48
Aristophanes 56, 92, 142
Aristotle 16, 18, 25, 34, 56, 117,
  121; *Poetics* 34
Arrabal, Fernando 115
Artaud, Antonin 119, 183
Arts Council of Great Britain,
  the 141
aside, dramatic 22, 176
As You Like It see Shakespeare,
  William
authorship 2, 50; authorial
  control 124, 138

Barbican Theatre, The Pit 114
Barthes, Roland 9, 15, 33, 99,
  101, 120, 183; 'Introduction
  to the Structural Analysis of
  Narratives' 15; 'Literature and

193